THE GREAT BRITISH
MOUNTAIN BIKE
TRAIL GUIDE

CLIVE FORTH

BLOOMSBURY
LONDON · NEW DELHI · NEW YORK · SYDNEY

CONTENTS

WALES

SCOTLAND

IRELAND

INTRODUCTION

Purpose built trails have been growing in popularity for nearly two decades, they have opened up the doors allowing more and more people to get onto two wheels and explore the stunning British countryside. This book is a guide to some of the classic and lesser-known trails that grace the Great British landscape, from the southern tip of England to the far flung corners of the Scottish Highlands via Wales and the Republic of Ireland, a mission that led to an epic journey and a wonderful insight into our island nation.

I recall a time when my friends and I used to banter on about the possibility of riding all the purpose-built trails in the UK in a day (and yes, it was possible). Now there are so many trails scattered across the British landscape it's impossible to ride them all in a month!

Those conversations were the driving force behind the creation of this book. I wanted to set myself an endurance-based challenge that people could relate to. As I'm not a marathon runner, it had to be centred around mountain biking. But what better way to see the great British landscape and celebrate 25 years of riding and racing bikes than a road trip?

With a busy schedule and a plethora of trails to choose from, I set my own target of riding 50 trails at various centres covering the far corners of the British Isles and Republic of Ireland in a month-long road trip. With friend and photographer Frazer Waller along for the ride, we set out on what became an epic and truly awesome road trip.

We hit the big names and rode a few hidden gems along the way. Unfortunately a couple of trails were closed for mainten-ance and we had to miss one or two of the well-known centres for logistical reasons. During the month-long road trip I rode just under 700km and the trusty VW covered nearly 7,000km. In total we spent 27 days on the road, 24 of which were riding days.

Planning and preparation is all part of the sport. To endure changing weather and trail conditions our journey involved many hours fettling bikes and watching weather reports. Whatever and wherever you're planning to ride, take care to ensure both you and your equipment are up to the task.

Pre-ride

Before you head out onto the trail it is important to make sure you have the correct equipment, it is well maintained and in good working order. Checking your equipment should be done in advance, preferably the day or night before. When planning a ride you should also take into account the following.

Weather conditions

Weather in mountainous regions (in fact pretty much anywhere you're likely to ride) can change very quickly, so always be prepared. Carry spares for your bike and extra clothing, including a wind and water-proof jacket. You may be riding at a bike park or purpose-built trail that is relatively close to communication, but do not be complacent: a rider who has crashed could go into a state of shock and your extra clothing layers could be the deciding factor in keeping them warm while waiting for help.

Most weather reports on television and radio are very basic and do not contain specific information to the region you will be riding. There are a multitude of websites for weather reports and regional phone numbers where you can get the most accurate up to date forecasts: just remember that even the professionals get it wrong from time to time.

Trail conditions

Hard-pack trails ride much faster than wet sodden ones. A wet trail will sap more energy; you will also have to lower your speeds when riding technical sections and your average speed will drop accordingly. The terrain, weather and distance of your ride will dictate what you should be carrying alongside your basic equipment. When riding in adverse conditions allow extra time to complete your ride.

COLOUR CODES FOR GRADES

▶ **Green** = easy family trails, mainly on wide open track with small hills and easy gradients.

▶ **Blue** = slightly narrower than green trails, longer in distance and may include technical trail features and purpose-built single-track sections.

▶ **Red** = technical trail features and increased elevation, gradient and exposure will be common on red grade trails; these trails are aimed at the real enthusiast.

▶ **Black** = exposed trails with longer distances, lots of technical trail features and steep gradients; aimed at riders with a high level of ability.

▶ **Orange** = signifies bike parks, jump spots etc; North Shore raised timber trails are common features on trails graded orange. Aimed at highly experienced and ambitious riders.

Time

How long will the route take? Always have a contingency plan in place. Leave details of your route with a family member or friend; make sure someone knows where you are going and when you intend to be back. Factor in any stops you will make and allow a bit of extra time for any potential mechanicals.

Equipment

You never know how long you may be out there; a string of mechanical problems could result in you being away from civili-sation for a much longer period of time than you had anticipated. Equally, it is essential to be well hydrated and nourished before going out on a ride, riding on an empty stomach will deplete you further from essential vitamins, minerals and nutrients.

Here's a list of the essentials you'll need for a safe and fun ride.

Your kit

- *First-aid kit*. I highly recommend the addition of super glue for sealing cuts, tampons for plugging up large bullet-type holes (brake levers and branches can create wounds of this nature), a mouthpiece for CPR, waterproof paper and pencil to record notes and rubber gloves for your personal protection.
- *Fluid*. Water with or without additives (sports drinks). You should drink approximately one litre per hour.
- *Maps*. Back up copied maps with a more detailed topographic map.
- *Multi-tool*. This should include a chain breaker, torques head keys, allen keys and screwdriver.
- *Tyre levers*. Some tyre/rim combinations may require levers. Good quality plastic ones are light yet robust, and are friendly on aluminium rims.
- *Spare inner tubes*. Make sure you have the correct valve. I carry Presta valve inner tubes as they fit all common rim styles.
- *Puncture repair kit*. Fast patches are easy to use as they do not need any glue making for a faster fix.
- *Tyre patch*. An old plastic toothpaste tube is ideal.
- *Tubeless tyre patch kit*.
- *Gaffer (or duct) tape*. Wind a length of tape onto a plastic card, this can be used to hold a tyre patch in place.
- *Pump*. Choose a good quality pump, my personal favourite is the Topeak Mountain Morph. Try to avoid storing this on the bike as it will be exposed to the elements, which may impede its performance. Look after your tools and they will look after you.
- *Spare mech hanger*. Most bikes now have replaceable rear derailleur hangers. They act as a failsafe, bending or breaking as opposed to the actual main frame being damaged.
- *SRAM quick links*. Make sure you get the correct link for your drive system, Gold = 9 speed, Silver = 8 speed or 10 speed).
- *Spoke key*. To fit your spoke nipples. There are various types so make sure your equipped with the correct tool.
- *Specialist tools and spares for your bike*.
- *Mobile phone*. Charged up with credit and switched off, it's advisable to store this in a dry sack.
- *Waterproof and windproof jacket*. On summer days and in hotter climates a lighter alternative outer layer may be more appropriate.

Optional additions for longer rides in more remote terrain. Tailor your kit to suit your ride.

- *Multi-tool*. With cutting implements, small adjustable spanner or mole-grips.
- *A mixture of bolts, nuts and washers*. You can take these from old worn out components, best stored in a dry sack.
- *Shock pump or shock replacement shock pump*.
- *Brake cable*. For those of you using cable-operated brakes.
- *Electrical connector*. For repairing a broken gear or brake cable.
- *Gear cable*. Make sure it's a rear, this will work on a front mech also.
- *Cable ties*. Also known as tie wraps or zip ties.
- *Replaceable spokes*. These will only work with traditional hub and rim systems.

● *Replacement for broken pedal axle.* A coach bolt with two washers and nut makes for a quick fix.

Trail etiquette

While you are out on the trail, be it a wilderness ride or a trail centre hack, it's likely that you will come across other riders and different trail users: the countryside is there for everyone's enjoyment not just yours. I'm sure you wouldn't want anyone to spoil your day out, or put you and your friends in danger, so please ride responsibly and treat other riders and trail users with respect.

Mountain bikes ridden in a controlled manner are generally quite quiet and have little impact on the environment, this makes it very easy to scare walkers, horse riders and other wildlife. When approaching other trail users slow down and politely greet them with a hello or good morning/good afternoon, take your time to pass them and give them plenty of space where possible. On super tight single-track trails it may be advisable to stop and stand off the trail. This may not be possible in all situations: steep gradients, loose surfaces and rough terrain make it hard to slow down. In these circumstances, control your speed and only let the pace build where good sight-lines allow you to do so. I have been in a good few of these situations myself and it's not nice, but this is one rare instance where the pedestrian should yield to the mountain biker.

When riding in a group give each other plenty of space so you can spot your ride line. Changes in pace can cause bottlenecks and a section that could be ridden with ease becomes a walk.

Purpose-built trails

Trail centres and bike parks are getting busier as more people take to the trails. You may have a faster rider catch you up or you may well catch up with a slower rider, once again control your speed and greet them with a polite hello. The known call in the UK race scene is 'rider' or 'rider up', I have also heard 'track' or just plain left and right called out. These call signs indicate that a faster rider is approaching and wishes to pass. Always give plenty of notice and if you are the slower rider make plenty of room as soon as you can to allow the faster rider to pass. If you are the faster rider be patient and wait for a good space before you attempt to overtake, a rash decision could result in an unnecessary accident.

Trailside manners

At some point in a ride it may be necessary to stop. Your bike may need fixing or you may just want a break for some nutrition and to appreciate the view. When stopping during a ride make sure you stand well off the trail and ride line, remove your bike from the trail and avoid laying it with the gears facing the ground. I have been in a few situations where groups of riders and their bikes are strewn across the trail round a blind turn. Fortunately I have been able to respond in time and avoid a nasty collision. We are all out for similar reasons and no one wants a premature end to their enjoyment. You wouldn't park your car in the middle of a main road, would you?

When carrying out repairs take your time, be methodical in your approach and take care not to lose items in long grass. Always take your old inner tubes and parts with you and leave no trace of having been there. Some fruits like bananas can take a long time to decompose so take the skin or pith with you. This still applies if you are on a purpose-built trail. Remember: every hour that rangers spend picking up litter is an hour less building or maintaining the trails.

Common sense, common safety

Obey all signage. As most mountain bike trails are built in working forests and old quarries, there may be operations taking place that involve heavy machinery or explosives. Familiarise yourself with the symbols and key on the map and do not under any circumstances enter areas marked with DANGER! Firing ranges and hunting zones can be active, there may be undetonated explosives on the ground, in quarries they could be using explosives or there may be unstable cliff faces. Foresting operations will involve heavy machinery and should also be avoided. Read the signs, follow diversions and keep an eye on what's around you and where you are on the map.

RIDING IN A RESPONSIBLE MANNER

Give way to other trail users

Be polite and courteous

Respect the rules of the road

Avoid skidding

Stick to the trail as best you can

Giving way to faster riders as soon as you can and do not intimidate slower riders

Standing off the trail when resting or working on your bike

Taking your rubbish with you

Trail information

For each trail centre there is a preceding information box providing an Ordnance Survey grid reference and the respective Ordnance Survey map to use to locate the centre, plus a sat nav reference.

The trails centres and the individual trails are rated in terms of how appropriate or enjoyable they are for riders at three levels: beginners, or those fairly new to blasting through single-track forest trails and breakneck downhills; intermediate riders, who have been mountain biking for a while now and are ready to take on pretty much any trail; and advanced riders, who would prefer a challenging trail at all times. The rating for each skill level is provided as a score out of 10. A score between 1/10 and 5/10 means the trails won't be much fun for your skill level. There might be fantastic trails with this score, it's just they're either too tough or not challenging enough for you. If the score is between 8/10 and 10/10 it's definitely a trail (or trail centre) for you. A 6/10 trail is good, but perhaps pushing at the comfort zone of a beginner, or a little too unchallenging for an intermediate or advanced rider. A 7/10 trail is definitely appropriate for your grade, but just falling short of being the perfect ride.

Trails also receive the standard blue, red, black or orange grade (see page viii) in two forms: the trail centre's grade and 'Clive's grade'. Having ridden them all, this latter grading is fully comparable across the book.

ENGLAND

ASTON HILL – WENDOVER WOODS

▶ **FACILITIES**

Car park and charges: Yes; free with permit

Cafe: No

Toilets: Yes

Showers: No

Bike wash: No

Nearest bike shop: Buckingham Bikes, Buckingham Street, Aylesbury, Bucks. HP20 2LE (01296 482077)

Bike hire: No

Accommodation: B&B, hotels in nearby Aston Clinton, Tring and Wendover.

Other trails on site: Downhill and 4X track, permissive paths and forest roads.

Ordnance Survey map: Explorer 181.

ENJOYMENT FOR SKILL LEVEL

Beginner: 5/10

Intermediate: 6/10

Advanced: 7/10

Permits: You can book a day pass or become a member on the Aston Hill website.

Getting there: Located south of the B4009 between the villages of Aston Clinton, Halton and Wendover. A sign from the B4009 points you up the steep hill. Go past the first forest entrance on your right and continue round the corner past the golf club entrance on your left. As you near the crest of the hill you will see the car park on your left-hand side. Please note the gates are locked around 5.30 p.m.

Grid ref: SP 89245 10140

Sat nav: HP22 5NQ

More info: www.rideastonhill.co.uk

Aston Hill was one of the original Forestry Commission sites developed for mountain biking in the British Isles. Mike and Ian Warby of Firecrest MTB worked in partnership with Forestry to develop a network of cross country and downhill mountain bike trails. The area is steeped in mountain bike history and back in the mid-1980s was home to some of the first mountain bike races in the British Isles. Going further back in time, riders from the Rough Stuff Fellowship used to roam around these forests in the 1950s on their Klunkers. Although the hills here are not particularly large, it's not an easy place to ride: the gradients are steep and the trail makes full use of the hillside and will challenge even the most competent rider.

Jumps and bermed corners run down the steep hillside on the 4X track

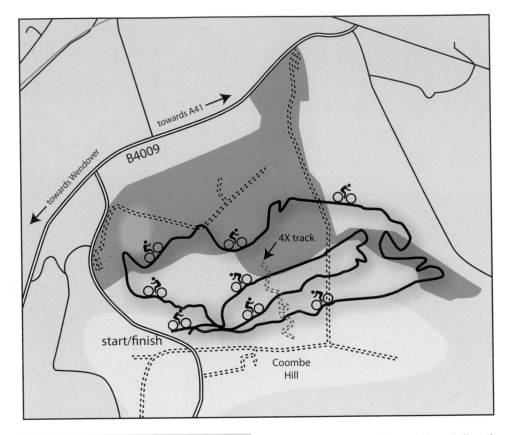

▶ XC BLACK TRAIL

On-site grade: Black

Clive's grade: Red with Black-grade sections

Distance: 5km

Technicality: 6/10

Ascent: 202m

ENJOYMENT FOR SKILL LEVEL

Beginner: 4/10

Intermediate: 5/10

Advanced: 6–7/10

The cross-country trails and downhill trails all start from an area just a few metres east of the main car park. All trails are well signed and easy to follow, however, there are one or two sections on the cross-country course that could be considered a little vague.

Exit the car park heading east and dip down twisting through the wooden fence. After the second fence climb up to your right slightly, following the Black signs with the white XC logo. The cross-country trail heads out along the top of the hill running parallel to a dirt track and the boundary of the forest. The large roots and root beds through this section give you a good idea of what lies ahead.

Continue heading east, descending slightly, and cross over the lower section of the 4X track. Take care here as there may be riders descending at high speed from your right. Once you have passed over the 4X track there is a steep climb out of a bomb hole before the trail continues to descend, dropping down through a series of tight corners. There are a few small bomb holes in this section and you just start to find your feet before you enter the climb. The trail traverses the upper slopes and heads back towards the car park. Here the gradient is quite steep in sections. When you ride over the 4X track again, keep your eyes peeled to the left for oncoming riders.

Continue to climb on single track back up to the main junction near the car park where all trails start. You then start to descend on a superb section of flowing single track starting off with a bomb hole. Swing left through the bomb hole and pop out into single track. A few metres further down the trail the cross-country route splits left at a fork. Watch out for it: while the signage is good it can be hard to see when riding at speed. This section is off camber (the trail traverses a gradient with no support for your tyres) and crosses multiple root beds before descending steeply into a right–left switch-back; it's this section that you're about to drop into that gives the trail its grade. Take care in the wet: these corners are carved into the hill and the chalk base can become very slippery.

After the switchbacks the trail continues to descend quite steeply, and you will enter another series of switchbacks. Again please note that these can become very slippery in the wet. After the switchbacks you have the

Roots galore on the narrow cross-country trail

The ride line can become vague in the winter months and the surface super slippery

option of a right- or a left-hand trail: they are similar in technicality and will converge at the same point a few metres further along.

After a large bomb hole you will find more switchbacks. Take care not to enter this section too fast: the switchbacks drop down quite a steep gradient and include a sizeable root drop or two. After the switchbacks there is the option of riding a section of boardwalk. If you do so, be aware there is a steep drop off at the end of the boardwalk and the trail falls away before joining the main forest road at the bottom of the hill.

Turn right and follow the main trail with the golf course to your left. The trail will rise up a small steep climb before descending round the forest boundary with the golf course remaining on your left. At the end of this section you enter the main climb: this is quite a steep section of trail and it's worth saving some energy as there is still plenty more climbing ahead. After a series of switchbacks and a steep section you will come to a fork, the left line follows the forest boundary – you can shortcut this section by going straight ahead. If you take the left turn the trail dips down and then continues to climb up around the forest boundary with open ground to your left. At the end of the section, you join a forest road that traverses the hill; continue to climb up before taking a left turn up off of the forest road (NB: this forest road is not surfaced). At this point the shortcut joins in from your right. Continue to climb up the hill. The trail will twist around before joining another double track.

Take a left turn onto this double track and after a few metres a tight right switch-back climbs up a bank and onto the boundary trail, there will be a fence to your left. Follow this trail along the top of the hill and you will arrive back at the start gate of the 4X track. The trail here lacks signage: continue straight ahead over the start hump and pass through some small bomb holes. Continuing to head west, you will soon arrive back at the main start to the downhill trails where you can cut through the fence back to the car or continue to do another lap.

▶ DOWNHILLS

Clive's grade: Orange/Black

Distance: N/A

Technicality: 6–7/10

ENJOYMENT FOR SKILL LEVEL

Beginner: 6/10

Intermediate: 7/10

Advanced: 7/10

The downhill trails on Aston Hill consist of roots, drops, jumps, off camber, tight corners, and fast open sections. You will also encounter steep gradients and these trails really have been built and designed for downhill specific bikes and riders with a high level of experience. There are four main runs to challenge you and a short steep push up round the forest boundary allows you to get back up for another blast in no time. You will find more information in the car park and details can be found on the website.

▶ALSO WORTH RIDING

BLANDFORD FORUM – UK BIKE PARK

Downhill runs and 4X track

Camping, hotels and B&Bs in the area

Uplift service and bike hire available

Location: Heading north on the A350 towards Shaftesbury, turn left onto the A357 and head to Shillingstone. Take a left turn opposite the church and continue to a T-junction, then take a left and another left when the road forks. Parking is at the top of the hill.

Grid ref: ST 817093

Sat nav: Shillingstone

Info: www.ukbikepark.com

PENSHURST – PORC

Jumps, mini downhill tracks, 4X track

Camping, hotels and B&Bs in the area

Location: From the A26 heading towards Royal Tunbridge Wells, turn right after crossing the A21. Follow the B2176 towards Penshurst. In the village, turn left onto Fordcombe Road B2188. After crossing the river, turn right up Grove Road and PORC is on your left.

Grid ref: TQ 516427

Sat nav: TN11 8DU

Info: www.porc.uk.com

SURREY HILLS

Various ungraded single-track trails

Camping, hotels and B&Bs in the area

Location: The Surrey Hills are located to the south-east of Guildford and to the south-west of Dorking. From the M25 London Orbital exit at Junction 10 and head south towards Guildford on the A3. Exit after several kilometres onto the A247 (West Clandon), pass the golf driving range and join the A25 towards Dorking. You can take the first major right onto the A248 and park in the village of Albury or continue to the next major right and turn off towards the village Shere. In Shere take a right onto Sandy Lane and head south. Immediately after the railway turn left towards Burrows Cross, pass through the village and continue down the lane to Peaslake village.

Grid ref: TQ 08568 44773

Sat nav: Gu5 9RR

Info: http://www.mountain-bike-guiding. co.uk/

SWINLEY FOREST

Various ungraded single-track trails

Hotels and B&Bs in the area

Bike hire available on site, car parking visitor centre and toilets

Location: You will need to buy a permit to ride from The Look Out Discovery Centre which is located just off the A322 between the M3 (junction 3) and M4 (junction 4). The brown tourist signs for The Look Out Discovery Centre will direct you off the A322 onto the B3430 (Nine Mile Road), the centre car park is clearly signed.

Grid ref: SU 876661

Sat nav: RG12 7QW

Info: www.rideswinley.com

CANNOCK CHASE

▶ FACILITIES

Car park and charges: Yes; charges apply; gates close at 20:00

Cafe: Yes

Toilets: Yes

Showers: No

Bike wash: No

Nearest bike shop: On site

Bike hire: Yes

Accommodation: Hotel, B&Bs located around The Chase, Rugeley and Cannock have all the usual amenities.

Other trails on site: Red (short loop, Follow the Dog), natural trails, forest breaks and permissive paths.

Ordnance Survey map: Explorer 244.

ENJOYMENT FOR SKILL LEVEL

Beginner: 7/10

Intermediate: 10/10

Advanced: 6/10

Getting there: From Cannock head north on the A460 through Hednesford. You will drive through the edge of the forest with a railway running parallel on your left. Just before Flexley Green take a left turn switching back and passing under the railway. Follow the lane for just over 1km and take the third left in Slitting Mill opposite the public house. At the T-junction turn left again and in a few hundred metres turn left down another lane, the entrance to the car park is on your left.

Grid ref: SK 01928 17032

Sat nav: WS15 2UQ

More info: www.chasetrails.co.uk

▶ MONKEY TRAIL

On-site grade: Red (with Black options)

Clive's grade: Red

Distance: 22km

Technicality: 6/10

Ascent: 530m

ENJOYMENT FOR SKILL LEVEL

Beginner: 4/10

Intermediate: 10/10

Advanced: 6/10

Cannock Chase is another area in the south of England (the Midlands to be precise) that has a long heritage of mountain biking. I remember racing in these woods in the early 1990s and some of the areas that the trails run over passed under my wheels over 20 years ago. Although the chase is relatively flat the trail makes good use of the small hills, winding its way up and down between the various gullies that are the remnants of an ancient riverbed. Having once been underwater the surface is made up of sand and gravel and this can pose an interesting challenge on some of the tight turns and steep climbing sections. The trail also becomes incredibly slippery in the wet and very abrasive on your components.

From the main visitor centre the trail winds its way through a pine plantation. It's tight in the trees and riders who opt to use wide handlebars will have to take care as it's easy to clip them. The trail drops down through a series of undulations and tight turns before dropping across a main forest road.

Here a series of boulders lead you into a section of Boardwalk and into more single track. The surface has small undulations but it's relatively flat. There is a public road down to your left-hand side. Just after this the trail climbs up and in a few metres joins on to a forest road. The forest road con-

tinues to climb uphill (there used to be an extension on the left which was graded as a Black option, however it was closed at the time of riding). At the top of this forest road take a left turn into a single track.

This tight and twisty section is in an area made up of young pine trees. You'll come to a small opening in the trees after a series of log drops; here you can opt for the shorter or longer of the two trails. The route continues to twist its way through the trees then you arrive at another series of log drops; once again you can roll over all of these and there's no need to launch off them. This section concludes in a series of switchbacks. The surface here is very loose and roots protrude so you will need to take care when navigating your way down the hill.

You are now on a disused road and you have the option of turning right and

Trailhead signage is clear and obvious

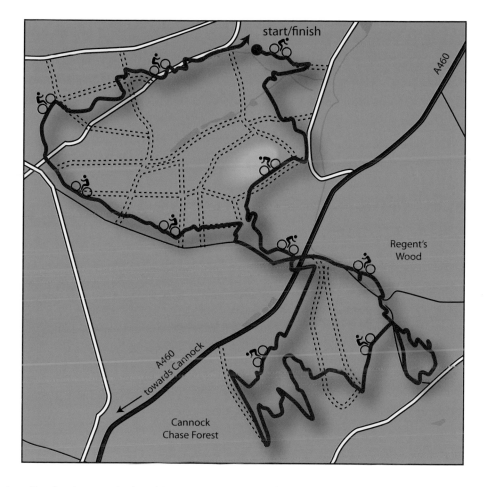

heading back towards the visitor centre or continuing on the longer loop by taking a left turn and dropping down to the railway and a level crossing. Make sure you dismount here and take care crossing over the railway line – this is a busy line and trains run relatively frequently!

After the railway line your next challenge is crossing over a busy main road: take your time and make sure it is safe to cross. Once on the other side of the road take a right turn and run along the tarmac section for just a few metres before turning left and climbing up a steep bank.

The surface is loose and the tight switch-backs make for a tough little climb. Once you cross the top of the hill the trail starts to descend, there were a few sections here where wide bars struggled to fit between the trees! The trail continues to traverse the hillside, mainly descending, and there are some great flowing turns. It's worth a note of caution at this stage: even in the dry your tyres will struggle to find traction on the loose shiny stones and sandy surface.

At the end of this section of single track there is a climb up on to a double track/ forest road, and the gradient increases as

The untreated boardwalk may be slippery when wet

you progress along this climb. This leads you up into a pine plantation and a classic Cannock single track, twisting its way through the trees.

The next couple of kilometres are a combination of twisting single track and forest roads/breaks. You'll come to a point in a single track where you have a split-line option, a Black-grade section to your left and Red-grade section continues to the right. The Black section comprises of rock drops, tight switchbacks and steep gradients. I feel the grading here is fair and it's only worth taking on this section of trail if you're confident in this type of terrain.

Having dropped down the steep hillside you will eventually rejoin the Red trail and climb back up. At the end of this section you drop down a break. At the bottom there is a T-junction onto another forest road. Here

the trail surface is loose so be careful not to let the speed pick up too much as you need to take a tight right turn and start to climb.

At the time of riding the section that followed was closed so we had to take a diversion. Local riders have told me that the trail continues in the same vein with single track and forest road/breaks linking to where I re-picked up the main loop. The signage seems pretty good up to this point so hopefully you shouldn't have too many issues navigating your way round.

I rejoined the trail climbing up a series of switchbacks on single track. The gradient is fair and it's easy to maintain a good pace through the turns. You join a shared trail for a few metres before taking a left and continuing on single track. The trail snakes its way along the ridge line, descending as it goes through mature pine trees, which become more sparse as you travel through this section. At a left-hand switchback you get a fleeting glance out across Cannock Chase. This is one of the highest areas in the Chase and it's well worth taking a moment to stop descending and savour the view.

From here on in the trail twists its way down the hillside. There are multiple drops, some of which are graded Black, and loose turns and switchbacks also keep you on your guard. Once again the surface is loose so decrease your speed here to avoid sliding out. A forest road link joins another section of single track where you climb up a few switchbacks, the trail then starts to descend and this leads you back towards the road crossing. There are a few junctions, the signage is great and it's very easy to navigate your way back to the main road where you headed on the outbound loop.

Cross the road and the railway line with care and climb up the disused road to a junction at the top. The shorter loop joins in from your right at this stage and the old road turns into a forest track. The remainder of the trail is a mixture of forest breaks linking single-track sections, there is minimal elevation gain and loss throughout the sections but the small steep gradients still require some effort. Unfortunately, during our ride for the book, we encountered some more diversions and simply followed forest breaks and forest roads back to the visitor centre. From previous visits to Cannock I recall the final sections of single track having a similar feel and flow as the outbound sections, but who knows what treats the trail builders have in store for you?

Make sure you take care when crossing the railway line. Dismount and walk your bike across

Stone-pitching on the Black option

►ALSO WORTH RIDING

DELAMERE

Two waymarked cross country loops: 6km Hunger Hill Trail and 11km Whitemoor Trail, skills area and various natural trails

Camping, hotels and B&Bs in the area

Bike shop, bike hire cafe and toilets on site

Location: Take the A51 from Chester towards Nantwich, take a left onto the A54 following signs to Manchester, after a few kilometres take a left onto the A556 to Delamere, in town turn left onto the B5152 and the trailhead is located near the train station.

Grid ref: SJ 548704

Sat nav: CW8 2JD

Info: www.forestry.gov.uk

SHERWOOD PINES

Cross-country trails, 4.8km Green, 9.6km Blue, two Purple routes and a 10km Red route

Camping, hotels and B&Bs in the area

Bike shop, bike hire cafe and toilets on site

Location: Take the A6030 heading north-east from Mansfield towards Clipstone. Pass through Clipstone and Old Clipstone, just after you pass under the railway bridge turn right into Sherwood Pines.

Grid ref: SK 612637

Sat nav: NG21 9JL

Info: www.forestry.gov.uk

CHICKSANDS – ROWNEY WARREN

▶ FACILITIES

Car park and charges: Yes; free with permit

Cafe: No

Toilets: No

Showers: No

Bike wash: No

Nearest bike shop: Bedford has a selection of cycle shops

Bike hire: No

Accommodation: B&Bs and hotels in Shefford, Cardington and Bedford.

Other trails on site: There are a multitude of natural trails around the woods; the north end is where all the action is and the south side is a no-cycle area.

Ordnance Survey map: Explorer 208.

ENJOYMENT FOR SKILL LEVEL

Beginner: 7/10

Intermediate: 5/10

Advanced: 5/10

Permits: Day tickets costing £5.00 can be purchased from a course manager on arrival, these are required on all days of the week including holiday periods. Or you can buy an annual membership:

Senior (16+): £60.00

Junior (15 or under): £40.00

Family (max 2 junior & 2 senior): £120.00

Getting there: Rowney Warren/ Chicksands trails and jumps are located a mile west of Shefford just north of RAF Chicksands. There are two car parks, located off the A600: the first one as you approach from Shefford is down a side road on your left and is a good start for taking in the XC loop; the second car park is further along the A600 at the end of the wood on Northwood End Road. This is the bikers' car park and a better location to park if you just want to ride the Jumps.

Grid ref: TL 11470 41575

Sat nav: Chicksands

More info: www.chicksandsbikepark.co.uk

▶ XC TRAIL

On-site grade: Red

Clive's grade: Blue with less than 10% Red sections

Distance: 7km

Technicality: 3.5/10

Ascent: 112m

ENJOYMENT FOR SKILL LEVEL

Beginner: 8/10

Intermediate: 6/10

Advanced: 4/10

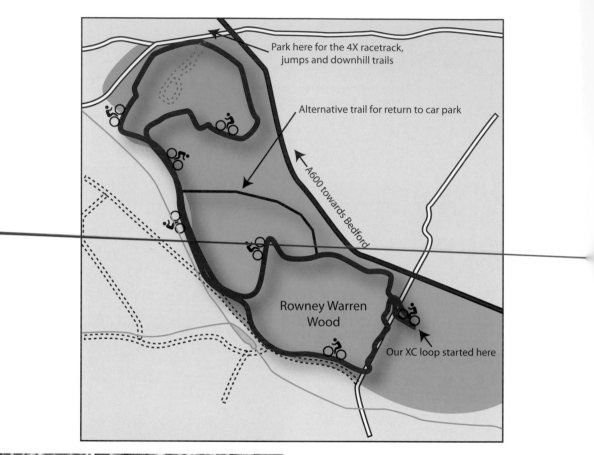

Park here for the 4X racetrack, jumps and downhill trails

Alternative trail for return to car park

A600 towards Bedford

Rowney Warren Wood

Our XC loop started here

There are a multitude of natural trails in the area, but unfortunately the signs for the original Red loop have now been removed, making it hard to navigate around the forest. From the car park at Northwood End Road follow the boundary with the road to your left. You will notice on your right-hand side various single-track trails disappearing off down the hillside. You can pick up any one of these trails and, keeping the

You never know who you may meet out on the trail. I bumped into an old friend (Mark Lee Sing – right) at Chicksands and we hit the dual course for some head-to-head racing action.

A tight single track follows the forest boundary

boundary to your left. At this point the trail starts to dip downwards through a gully and there are some interesting narrow sections with stumps, roots and low-slung trees to navigate around. The trail then bears to the right and dips down, crossing a walker's path in the bottom of the dip. You should take care when approaching this section!

To your left, the single track continues running parallel to the boundary fence, which is next to open fields. After a few hundred metres you will come to a fork in the trail. Keep left here, and the trail enters some tightly packed trees before climbing up with houses to your left. As you crest the hill you come onto a forest break where you need to take a left then a right turn into

another section of single track. You will now be near the 4X car park with a country lane (Northwood End Road) to your left. To get back to the start point either retrace your steps or head south-east with the main A600 to your left.

A lap of the boundary is approximately 7km long. You can make your ride much longer by criss-crossing the forest using the network of single-track trails that have developed over the years. The forest only covers a small area and is easy to navigate around.

Be aware in the summer months as there will be more users, caution should be taken at the bottom of each descent as there is usually a multi-user trail crossing over at this point.

▶JUMP PARK AND DOWNHILLS

Clive's grade – jumps and downhills: Orange/Black

Distance: N/A

Technicality – jumps: 6–10/10

Technicality – downhills: 5–7/10

JUMPS: ENJOYMENT FOR SKILL LEVEL

Beginner: 4/10

Intermediate: 7/10

Advanced: 9/10

DOWNHILLS: ENJOYMENT FOR SKILL LEVEL

Beginner: 7/10

Intermediate: 5/10

Advanced: 4/10

The 4X track, jump spot, and dual slalom tracks are located opposite the car park on the Northwood End Road. Here you will find a multitude of lines to choose from including a 4X racetrack, dual slalom track, and multiple dirt jump lines. This area of the forest is fenced off and is exclusively for bikes. You will find some very challenging sections within this area of the forest but the forgiving nature of the soil means you can play to your heart's content and progress in relative safety.

There is also a series of downhill tracks. The Bull Run starts with a 3-metre-high drop and is a very fast track that takes you through bomb holes and incorporates large jumps and some tight turns. Another track, the Snake Run, starts in the same place as The Bull Run. This trail has sweeping berms, large gaps, moguls and rooted sections. This is another fun, although short, downhill trail.

Tom Dowie coaches a rider through bermed turns on the 4X track

DALBY FOREST

► FACILITIES

Car park and charges: Yes; charges apply

Cafe: Yes

Toilets: Yes

Showers: No

Bike wash: Yes

Nearest bike shop: On site

Bike hire: Yes

Accommodation: Camping, B&Bs, lodge houses, hotels in and around the area.

Other trails on site: Green, Blue, jump park and skills area; permissive routes and forest roads.

Ordnance Survey map: Explorer OL27.

ENJOYMENT FOR SKILL LEVEL

Beginner: 7/10

Intermediate: 8/10

Advanced: 7/10

Getting there: From the A169 Pickering to Whitby Road turn off by the Fox and Rabbit pub onto Thornton-le-Dale Road. To get to the trail-head follow the forest drive for a couple of kilometres. To ride the Red, Blue and Green trails you can park at the main visitor centre. For the jump spot, skills area and World Cup racetrack continue along the forest drive for another couple of kilometres to Dixon's Hollow. You will see the jump spots to your right and there is ample parking to the left of the Forest Road.

Grid ref: SE 88446 89758 (Dixon's Hollow car park)

Sat nav: YO18 7LT

More info: www.forestry.gov.uk/dalbyforest

► TRAIL 1. WORLD CUP XC (STARTING AT DIXON'S HOLLOW)

On-site grade: Black

Clive's grade: Red with Black sections

Distance: 4.5km

Technicality: 7/10

Ascent: 166m

ENJOYMENT FOR SKILL LEVEL

Beginner: 3/10

Intermediate: 7/10

Advanced: 9/10

The Black-graded World Cup racetrack was built with one thing in mind: racing! The trail may be short but it will test you. The surface at Dalby is very sandy and is hard on your components; it also makes for some tricky riding.

The opening section of the World Cup track flows through a nice piece of single track, descending ever so slightly. Beyond the small trees is a series of whoops and some flowing turns. Be careful as the loose surface makes it hard to find grip and the speed is quite high at this point.

You will exit the single track onto a forest road. The trail then takes a right turn up a large piece of rock. This requires quite a high level of commitment as the trail beyond it is hidden from sight and the face of the rock is quite steep. A short section of single track runs parallel to the forest road before rejoining it for approximately 20m. Here the Red route continues on the forest road but the World Cup track takes a right turn and climbs up once more.

At the top of the climb you will find a section of boardwalk. When you exit the boardwalk there is a split-line option with the Red-grade section to your right and a Black-grade section to your left. The Black-grade section runs down some boulders that are set in the floor but is relatively easy.

Another short descent leads you back to the forest road. There is a split-line option to join the forest road and the right-hand line has a sizeable rock drop – it is possible to roll down on the left-hand side. The forest road only lasts for a few metres before a left turn drops you into the gully.

This section has some roots and rocky drops and you will pass through the bottom of the gully with another split-line option. To your right is a Black option, which comprises of a steep drop-in. You

Clear signage warns you of drop offs

The large drop off into the gully on the World Cup track. Take care here as the run out is limited

can also opt for the Red-line option, which switches its way down into the bottom of the gully.

The trail then runs along the bottom of a deep gully where the surface is quite loose and rough and the speed quite high. There are option lines to your right if you want some more challenging drops.

As the gradient eases the trail has a fork where you need to take a left turn and enter a bermed turn to the right; you then pass back over the trail climbing up a steep bank. It is quite a confusing junction and the signage is not great at this point, so make sure you climb up on the right-hand side of the gully/valley.

At the top of this section you will rejoin the Red trail. Take care here as riders on the Red trail will be descending on quite a steep gradient and may be approaching at speed!

The gully is loose and fast

Traverse across the hillside on a nice flowing piece of single track before turning left and descending down the steep bank following the signs for the Black trail. The descent is only short but relatively technical: the trail surface is loose and there are some drop-offs to deal with as you switch down the hillside.

You roll out the bottom of the descent and then turn right onto a trail that leads you around the bottom of this hill before another right turn into a climb. You will see the Red trail disappear off to the left at this point.

The gradient on the climb is quite steep but don't fear for it doesn't last too long. At the top you take a right turn and run along a nice natural piece of trail with open ground to your left. The trail then bears to the right and starts to descend; this section is very natural with a few roots and rocky drops to keep you entertained.

At the bottom of this small descent you join on to a forest road where you take a left turn; you will now be traversing around the opposite side of the gully where you dropped in earlier.

The trail drops in and cuts through the bottom of the gully once more, on the far side is a short sharp steep climb, this climb has a split-line option, the line on the right switches up the hill and the left option has three sizeable steps to deal with. Whichever line you take, you will rejoin a forest road and continue to climb straight ahead.

The trail then turns right and away from the forest road and traverses across the top of the hill passing back over the boardwalk area. A short flowing section leads you back to the car park and the trailhead where you started the loop.

▶TRAIL 2. RED (STARTING AT DIXON'S HOLLOW)

On-site grade: Red

Clive's grade: Red

Distance: 34km

Technicality: 6/10

Ascent: 616m

ENJOYMENT FOR SKILL LEVEL

Beginner: 3/10

Intermediate: 7/10

Advanced: 6.5/10

I started my Red lap having done a warm-up loop on the World Cup track. The trail heads out on the same route as the World Cup trail. When you join the forest road continue around the hillside before dropping into the gully, the World Cup track turns off to your left and the Red route continues to climb up on the far side of the gully.

The trail twists and winds its way along the gully edge. Dropping down and climbing up slightly, you will descend down the hillside through a series of tight and loose switchbacks before rejoining the World Cup trail.

The Red trail now drops in to your left and descends down through another series of switchback turns. You ride along the valley base then a left turn climbs up the hillside through a series of switchbacks. Once again the trail surface is relatively loose and you can tell that on a wet day the surface would be very hard on your equipment.

At the top of this climb, keep to the right at a fork and join a double track. This double track is quite natural and there is

Freshly built tabletop jumps at Dixon's Hollow

evidence that it becomes wet and boggy during the winter months. You will now have a few kilometres of forest roads and a few junctions to negotiate, the trail is well signposted and you should have no issues at all in navigating your way.

You will also run along a section on the hilltop which has stunning views out to your left. Along this section there is the option to follow a shortcut out to your right; the main trail continues straight on passing around a gate. After a short while you will turn right off of the forest road and into a single track. This section is fast, the trail surfaces are smooth: take care as some of the corners tighten up on themselves.

Another forest road link leads you to the next section of single track. Once again the signage is great and there should be

Good tyre choice will help you find some grip on the woodwork. Take extra care in the wet

no issues at all in finding where you're going. The next single track starts to descend slightly. You'll pass over a section of boardwalk, cross a forest road and turn a hard left, following a single track running parallel to the forest road. The section has a few little crests and drops but nothing to fear.

You will cross over the main forest drive at Bickley Gate and continue straight ahead on more single track. At this stage in the trail there is little in the way of elevation loss and gain and the trail surface is quite chattery – it's like you're riding on cobbles at times.

The single tracks are split into sections crossing over forest roads and the forest drive; there are wooden pinch gates to slow you down and make you aware that you are about to cross them. After a few kilometres the forest drive, which you've been running parallel with, veers off to your right and you take a wide forest road to the left, along here you will have open lands to your left and the forest to your right.

This section of forest road lasts for just under 2km, there are a couple of junctions and the signage is good. You get your next section of single track on your right-hand side of the forest road, this section is raised up like a causeway and at the time we rode this track for the book it was newly built. The surface through this section is very smooth and it's easy to maintain a decent speed.

The trail does descend slightly and there are a few crests and whoops throughout this section. Crossing over a forest road through some pinch gates you start to climb up slightly. Still on a single track trail, you then descend into some deciduous trees.

Although there is not much gradient to this section of the trail you can maintain a decent speed, but bear in mind there is still a considerable distance to go and you may want to conserve your energy for the later climbs. Partway along this section was a tight bomb hole and it's worth slowing up in order to deal with compression in the bottom.

The gradient then steepens and you drop through some rocky switchbacks. It's these short sections and the distance that gives the trail its grade. Beyond the switchbacks you'll pass through another pinch gap fence – those of you with wider bars may find this one a bit of a squeeze!

The trail runs down a forest road before turning right and climbing up the hillside. Then a section of switchbacks, descents and climbs up out of a small valley becomes a running theme for the next several kilometres. Some of the switchback sections you will encounter while descending are quite rough and loose; there is also one section after a left-hand switchback in a descent that has a few drop-offs. But there is nothing too severe, and if you have ridden the technical sections prior to this you should have no problems.

A flowing section of single track leads you through some large pine trees. On the left you will see the link trail that connects the track to the main visitor centre, but continue to traverse around the hillside heading back up towards Dixon's Hollow. The final stages of the trail climb and descend, some sections of trail are quite loose and if you're tired you may find these a bit of a challenge. The final few kilometres of trail are predominantly uphill, so for this reason it may be worth considering starting the Red trail from the visitor centre so at least you finish your ride with the descent. A wide track climbs up and when you see the skills area/jump line on your left you know you're home and hopefully dry. The car park is just over to your left, past the jumps.

Rocks and roots on the return leg to Dixon's Hollow

FOREST OF DEAN

▶FACILITIES

Car park and charges: Yes; charges apply

Cafe: Yes

Toilets: Yes

Showers: Yes

Bike wash: Yes

Nearest bike shop: On site

Bike hire: On site

Accommodation: Camping, B&B, hotels in and around the forest. The nearby towns of Coleford and Cinderford have shops, restaurants and petrol stations.

Other trails on site: Yellow family trail, bridleways.

Ordnance Survey map: Explorer OL 14.

ENJOYMENT FOR SKILL LEVEL

Beginner: 8/10

Intermediate: 6/10

Advanced: 5/10

Getting there: On the B4226 Coleford to Cinderford road head north at the crossroads with the B4234 and follow the brown signs to the Cycle Centre.

Grid ref: SO 60840 12431

Sat nav: GL16 7EH

More info: www.1sw.org.uk

▶TRAIL 1: VERDERERS TRAIL

On-site grade: XC Blue 'Verderers trail'

Clive's grade: Blue with Red sections

Distance: 10.5km

Technicality: 5/10

Ascent: 240m

ENJOYMENT FOR SKILL LEVEL

Beginner: 7/10

Intermediate: 6/10

Advanced: 5/10

From the main car park the trailhead is quite vague. With the cafe to your left, head round to the right up to the top corner of the car park where the skills area heads out up to your left and the Blue trail leads out up to the right-hand side. There you will join a forest road where the signs are quite vague: continue to follow the forest road at the junction, take a right turn and stick to the forest road for the next 750m. Turn

Great signage at Forest of Dean thanks to the 1 Southwest project

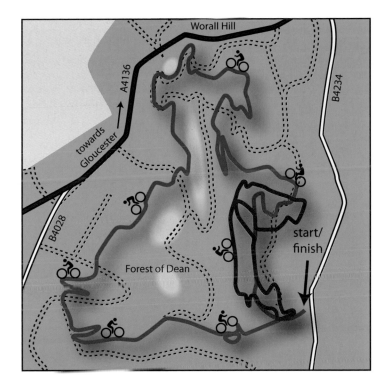

right into single track. Take care through this section as there are some bermed corners and whoops in the trail. At the end of this section you will take a left turn and join a forest road. Further along this forest road, turn left into single track, here the trail starts to climb upwards. This section is quite steep for a Blue-grade trail and there are a couple of uphill switchbacks to negotiate as you continue to traverse the hillside before dropping down a relatively steep section of trail.

At the start of this descent there is a Red option line. This section can become very greasy and caution is needed on the steep bermed turns. The Red Line rejoins the Blue trail and continues to drop downhill through a series of whoops and tight turns before climbing up on the other side of the hill. The trail surface is quite rough in places

and feels like you're riding on cobbles, although a good-quality suspension bike will remove the high-frequency buzz that you get from the trail's surface.

The single track joins into a forest road, which has been surfaced on the left-hand side; the right-hand side could become muddy in the winter months. At the top of the climb the trail switches round to the left and traverses along in among deciduous trees before turning right into a single-track section that loops around on the hilltop.

The trail descends and drops you down before running parallel to a forest road. It can get quite muddy through this section! The trail then turns right and climbs up through a set of switchbacks before levelling out as it crosses the hilltop.

The single-track trail will eventually come to a forest road where you cross

The switchback climb gets you up fast

straight over. This is the area where the downhill trail starts; your Ordnance Survey map will be marked as edge end. Through this next section the trail descends slightly and will join a forest road where you climb up for a few metres before turning right into the start of the final descent.

The final descent is quite lengthy and the top section involves some peddling before you blend into the main downhill trails in the lower half of the hill. Save some energy for the large whoops, jumps and compressions that lay ahead.

This section of trail is closer to Red grade and the less-experienced riders among you should take caution through this section. It is also much busier in this area of the forest and you may encounter other riders at the bottom of their downhill runs. A split-line option in this section gives you the option to take a Red line on the right or a Blue line to the left. At the bottom of this downhill

the trails converge and go through the gully that you followed on your outbound trail. From here just roll back into the car park and you have completed your lap.

▶TRAIL 2. FREEMINER TRAIL

On-site grade: Red 'Freeminer Trail'

Clive's grade: Red

Distance: 4.5km

Technicality: 6/10

Ascent: 113m

ENJOYMENT FOR SKILL LEVEL

Beginner: 6/10

Intermediate: 7/10

Advanced: 5/10

Trailhead signage and outbound signage. The Red trail starts over the rocks next to the sign marked START

Starting from the same location as the Blue trail described above, the Freeminer trail climbs up onto a bank where the Blue trail heads out along the gully. There is quite a large hole in one of the drops at the start of this trail and the section that follows through the trees is quite rooty and will become slippery on wet days.

The single-track trail comes to a forest road where you will go straight over, continuing into another single-track section. The trail switchbacks and climbs up, traversing the hillside before crossing another forest road. On the far side of the forest road the trail forks left and runs around the edge of a large bomb hole and starts to climb up. At the top of the climb the trail then starts to descend. You will cross another forest road where the narrow single-track trail continues to descend. This section has some great corners and root beds, just look out for the stump on the exit of a right-hand berm!

Root beds may be more challenging in the wet. Keep right at this split in the trail

You will start to climb back up again. Here there are a few desire lines that cross the main trail, but stay on the main obvious trail. You will pass over a section of boardwalk before crossing over another forest road climbing up into open ground. Cross the open ground with a fence to your left-hand side and climb up into a plantation of large pine trees where the trail will turn left and descend through a gully. There are multiple lines here too: don't panic if you get off the main line as they all lead in the same direction. You can make up whichever variation of the gully run you desire.

Nearing the end of the single-track section there is quite a cheeky dip before you join a forest road. Here there is currently no signage! Take a right turn down the forest road where you will come to a crossroads, you will have a section of

The trail feels very natural and looks great with spring starting to bloom

single track to your left, once again the signage is vague.

This section of single track winds its way around the back of the council depot before leading you back towards the car park. There are a few sections here that become wet and sticky during the winter months and you may come across other trail users, as this is where all trails return back to the main car park.

▶DOWNHILL TRAILS

Clive's grade: Orange/Black

Distance: N/A

Technicality: Downhills, 5–6/10

ENJOYMENT FOR SKILL LEVEL

Beginner: 6/10

Intermediate: 7/10

Advanced: 6/10

There are a few established downhill runs, all of which are relatively short. You may encounter jumps, drops, roots and steep gradients in the downhill trails. There is an uplift service that runs daily and you can pay for single runs. There are many desire lines and unofficial trails in the area: the majority of the lines come down the right-hand side of the hill and the steeper lines run down the left-hand side. You will find more information on site, and the friendly folk in the bike shop will be only too happy to help.

GISBURN – FOREST OF BOWLAND

►FACILITIES

Car park and charges: Yes; free

Cafe: No

Toilets: No

Showers: No

Bike wash: No

Nearest bike shop: ATR Cycles, Whalley Industrial Park Clitheroe Road, Barrow, Clitheroe BB7 9AH (01254 825 896)

Bike hire: No

Accommodation: B&Bs, hotels in and around the area.

Other trails on site: Blue, Black freeride/jump line, forest roads and permissive paths.

Ordnance Survey map: Explorer OL41.

ENJOYMENT FOR SKILL LEVEL

Beginner: 5/10

Intermediate: 10/10

Advanced: 9/10

Getting there: Take the A65 heading south from Settle. Just before the junction with the A682 at Long Preston take a right turn onto the B6478 to Slaidburn. After the village of Wigglesworth you need to take a right at the second set of crossroads, there are signs at this junction pointing down the narrow lane, the car park will be on your right.

Grid ref: SD 74564 55046

Sat nav: Slaidburn

More info: www.gisburnbiketrails.com

►THE 8

On-site grade: Red

Clive's grade: Red

Distance: 17.5km

Technicality: 8/10

Ascent: 450m

ENJOYMENT FOR SKILL LEVEL

Beginner: 3/10

Intermediate: 9/10

Advanced: 9/10

From the car park, the trailhead signs lead out on a wide smooth track. The start to the trail is relatively flat and easy-going. At the end of the opening straight, bear left onto a forest road, where it descends slightly. At the bottom, bear right onto another forest road before taking a left turn and continuing to descend on forest roads. The route goes from forest road into a single track; the gradient is minimal

Always read the signs before you start, there may be diversions or key information you need to observe

The single track is easy-going and will bring you out next to a country lane. The trail runs parallel to the lane before joining on to the tarmac where you will cross over a bridge at the end of the lake. The view across the lake is spectacular although I could imagine it could be quite exposed here and windswept in the autumnal and winter months.

Just over the bridge the trail turns off to your right and you climb up on a single track. The climb is relatively easy and it's a nice warm up at the start of the ride. You will join a forest road once more and at the top of this section the single track heads off in front of you and starts to become more technical.

but the surfaces are loose. The dense trees in this section make it hard for the sun to penetrate, so be wary as it may be greasy through this part of the trail.

The trail's surface is quite rough in places through the single track and you will join a forest road taking a left turn. After a

A smooth start as the Red and Blue trails are shared at this stage

few metres, take a right turn into another twisting section of single track. At the end of the section there is a split-line option, both of which bring you onto a forest road. Here you turn right and cross over a stream.

The trail now continues to climb; take it easy as there are plenty more kilometres ahead. Partway along this section you will see trail signs off to your left, this is the return loop so stick to the forest road and continue to climb up slightly to a junction on your left.

Take the left turn and climb up. Here the gradient gets a bit steeper and you will have trees to your right and open grounds to your left. At the top of the climb the main Red route takes a left turn and on your right-hand side you have the Hope free ride/downhill line.

Traverse across the hillside on the forest road with spectacular views out to your left. You only have a few metres to appreciate the stunning views before turning right and climbing up through a disused quarry. This section is quite technical and gives you a taste of what lies ahead.

A short section of wide trail links you into Simon's Swamp. This section of trail traverses open moorland and there are large pieces of rock in the floor for you to ride over to avoid the boggy ground. The

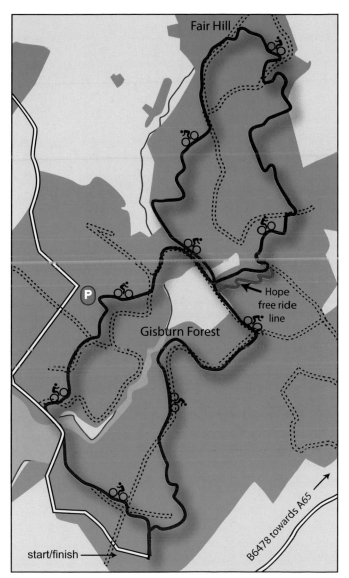

trail here is very rough and requires some serious power output in order to maintain a decent speed. Having crossed the open ground, you enter the treeline and the trail switchbacks as it climbs up the hillside. The surface is smoother and you will find it easy-going in comparison to the previous section.

Rock drop offs and loose surface provide a challenge

When you reach the top of this section you will once again have some spectacular views. Then the trail drops down slightly before climbing up to an exposed rocky outcrop. Here you have split-line options and there is a small Black loop that takes in the rocky outcrop. The Red trail twists its way around through the rocks and there are some jumps and drops to deal with, as well as some tight corners. A little climb completes this section before you start to descend.

After a short section of single-track descent you join into a forest road, taking a right turn and climbing up slightly. The trail drops off the forest road to your left into the section named Hully Gully. This section is fantastic fun – there are blind crests and jumps and a large gully creates huge natural berms that snake down the hillside. At the bottom of the gully the trail takes a left turn, crossing over a stream before climbing up a steep bank.

Climb up out of this section and join a forest road where you start to descend. Try and carry some speed on this descent as you take a left–right turn through the bottom of a dip and climb up on the far side of a small river. At the top of the short rise there will be a dry stone building to your right, which will offer you some shelter if you need to stop and take a break and the weather is not on your side.

Beyond the dry stone building you turn off the forest road and take a right turn onto a very natural section of trail. This descends ever so slightly, so just be aware that there are some tight holes in the trail and the odd soft patch. You will come out into the open and descend down a hillside. Here you encounter large root beds, rocks and rough ground. Take care through this section and choose your lines wisely. At the bottom of the descent climb up a short sharp steep bank before descending again through a series of sweeping turns down to a dry stone wall.

The trail runs alongside a dry stone wall before crossing through a stream and climbing up out onto a forest road. This forest track links you into a single-track trail and you are now running parallel to the forest road you took on your outbound

Rocky outcrops tower above the trail

loop. The section of single track is quite cheeky and has a few narrow boardwalks to navigate. After these you will pop out onto a forest road and descend.

The forest road starts to descend and you soon pick up some good momentum. The trail drops off the forest road to your right and you will be on a shared trail with the Blue loop. This section is fast and has some mellow turns that offer good grip. This section joins another forest road link to the next section of single track.

You're in the final stages of the ride and in this single-track section you will find a fork. Keep to the left and head into the trees, descending slightly as you do so. The final section of single track is quite greasy, so take care as you only have a couple of kilometres to go to complete the loop. From the forest road link the return section

of trail is the same section you started the ride on. This two-way trail will lead you back into the car park.

Natural rooty and rocky descents will give your arms and suspension a work out

GRIZEDALE

The woodman and his axe

▶ FACILITIES

Car park and charges: Yes; charges apply

Cafe: Yes

Toilets: Yes

Showers: No

Bike wash: Yes

Nearest bike shop: On site

Bike hire: Yes

Accommodation: B&Bs, hotels, campsites and youth hostels in and around the area of Hawkshead and Ambleside.

Other trails on site: Black DH trail, permissive paths and forest roads.

Ordnance Survey map: Explorer OL7.

ENJOYMENT FOR SKILL LEVEL

Beginner: 2/10

Intermediate: 8/10

Advanced: 9/10

Getting there: From Hawkshead make your way south, you will see a small narrow lane between houses and brown signs pointing you to Grizedale Forest. Climb up over the hill and after a few kilometres you drop down the other side and you will see the car park and visitor centre to your right.

Grid ref: SD 33421 94259

Sat nav: LA22 0QJ

More info: www.forestry.gov.uk/thenorthfacetrail

▶ THE NORTH FACE TRAIL

On-site grade: Red

Clive's grade: Red

Distance: 16.5km

Technicality: 7/10

Ascent: 342m

ENJOYMENT FOR SKILL LEVEL

Beginner: 4/10

Intermediate: 8/10

Advanced: 7.5/10

The trail starts by the bike shop below the visitor centre. Follow the gravel road around through the farm buildings and be aware of other trail users and oncoming traffic in this area. Just below the farmhouse you head through a five-bar gate and start to climb up on a forest road out in open ground.

The Forest Road takes a switchback right and climbs up for a few metres before you turn left into a single-track trail. The opening climb traverses around the hillside and is rough and technically challenging. Expect to encounter tight switchback and rocky outcrops. There are multiple desire lines that have appeared, evidence that riders have been pushing through this part of the trail, but try and avoid these and stick to the main trail.

When you exit the top of the single-track climb you will join a forest road and continue to climb for a short distance. The

Great signage at the start of a great trail

next section of trail is a flowing but rough piece of single track. This, however, is short-lived and you're back onto a forest road and climbing for some considerable distance.

At the top of the climb the forest road continues to run along the ridge lines and you have wonderful views down to

Rocky single track climbs up around the hill, tight switchbacks and lovely views

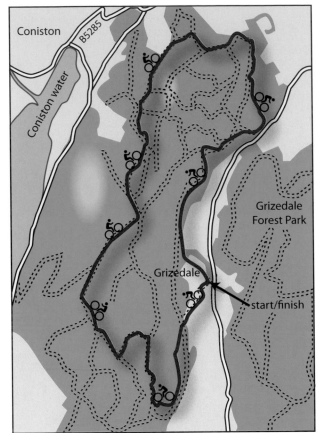

again at a high elevation. Within the sections of single track you will pass over a few boardwalks. It is advisable to take care on wet days as they can become very slippery!

The final section of single track in this leg joins the forest road with a switchback to your left and after a few metres you switch right into the next piece of trail. This is the only part on the trail where navigation and signage could cause a problem. You'll discover that the majority of the single tracks in Grizedale are rough and loose – but what else would you expect from the Lake District!

You join back into a forest-road-link section as you climb up and drop down, heading away from those spectacular views and back into the main forest. The following kilometres are a mixture of flowing single track and forest-road-link sections. You will have some relatively flat and rough sections of trail to deal with before passing the upper car park and heading into the final descent.

The final descent isn't particularly steep but you do get a good distance on single-track trail as you drop back down the hill towards the visitor centre.

There are a few sections in this final descent with very tight corners, so watch out for these. You will also have a final forest-road-link section and a long section of boardwalk to negotiate. The final stages of the descent are out in the open and a pair of gates split up the final section before you make it back to the visitor centre.

Coniston Water, and on a clear day you can also see The Old Man of Coniston towering above the village. The forest road dips down and climbs up and you will turn right into another piece of single track. Originally there was a boardwalk at this section but that has now been replaced with large stone sets to help you navigate your way through some wet and boggy ground.

You rejoin the forest road and continue to traverse along the hilltop. Once again you will leave the forest road and take a section or two of single track. These sections descend slightly but overall we are

Spectacular views over to Walna Scar and the Old Man of Coniston

HALDON - EXETER

►FACILITIES

Car park and charges: Yes; charges apply

Cafe: Yes

Toilets: Yes

Showers: Yes (key available from ranger)

Bike wash: No

Nearest bike shop: On site

Bike hire: Yes

Accommodation: B&Bs, hotels, camping and self-catering accommodation in area.

Other trails on site: Blue, Green.

Ordnance Survey map: Explorer 110.

ENJOYMENT FOR SKILL LEVEL

Beginner: 7/10

Intermediate: 6/10

Advanced: 5/10

Getting there: At the top of the hill on the main road (A38) follow the brown signs to Haldon Forest Park – the junction is also signed for Exeter racecourse. Follow the country lane for a few kilometres and you will see the main entrance to the Forest Park on your left.

Grid ref: SX 88427 84869

Sat nav: EX6 7XR

More info: www.forestry.gov.uk

Holden Forest Park is a Forestry Commission managed site. There are very few permissive paths within the forest, and so provision has been made for mountain bikes and walkers to enjoy the landscape. The mountain bike trails start from the visitor centre located on Buller's Hill. Holden Forest is a working forest and the landscape may have changed by the time you read this due to various felling operations, however, the commission have a responsibility to keep the trails open and any information regarding diversions or closures can be found on the commission's website.

►RIDGE RIDE TRAIL

On-site grade: Red

Clive's grade: Red with some easier Blue sections

Distance: 9.5km

Technicality: 6/10

Ascent: 203m

ENJOYMENT FOR SKILL LEVEL

Beginner: 7/10

Intermediate: 7/10

Advanced: 5–6/10

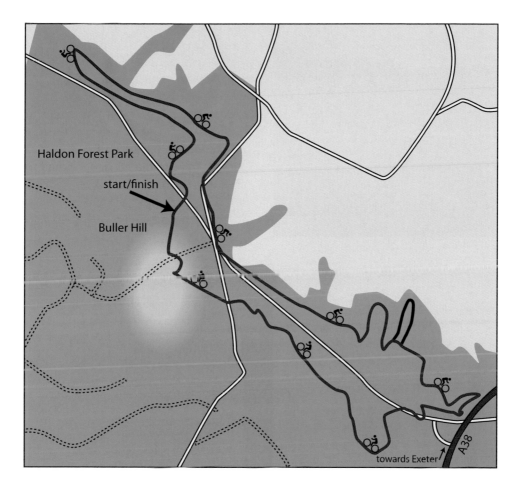

From the main car park cross over the country lane and join a forest road. After a few metres the trail forks off to the left. This section gives you a taste of what's to come, twisting turns with some tight bermed corners link rocky drops that lead you into more flowing corners before popping out onto a double track.

Here you have spectacular views across to your right back towards Exeter. However, the double track only last a few metres so enjoy the views while you can in safety. You will then take a right fork and into a single-track traverse. The trail now starts to

descend down the hill. Since there are a few tight blind corners within this section, take care as there is no support on the outside of these corners!

You will continue to descend before switching right and traversing back across the hillside. This section starts to climb slightly upwards but the gradient is easy-going. You will eventually end up next to a country lane on your left. The trail is cut into a steep hillside and has a fence to your left; the taller riders among you may want to take care in this section as there is an overhanging tree that you will have to duck

Sweet single track and stunning views

Rocks and roots keep you on your guard as the trail traverses the hillside

under. The single track drops left through a very tight pinch gate crossing the country lane. The next section descends and crosses over a couple of small bridges.

Cross over a footpath then take a left-hand switch and continue to descend, crossing the footpath once more. The trail runs around the hill with a forest road to your left. Traverse the hill and descend to join into this forest road where you will come to a large turning circle. At this point you can continue straight on along the forest road on the Red route or you have the option of a short Black section that drops in to your left down some steep stone-pitching.

The Black section is quite narrow and quite rough in places but is well worth a look if your skills are up to it. As you exit the switchbacks at the bottom of the Black descent you will join a double track that climbs back up. This double track joins into the turning circle where you will rejoin the Red route and continue to climb up around the front of the hill on a wide forest road. At the top of this forest road take a tight right-hand switchback where the trail continues to climb (now on single track) traversing the hillside. The next section is an interesting climb that leads you up onto the country lane. Take care crossing the lane: although small it is quite a busy road!

On the other side of the road you will enter another twisting section of trail, which is cut into a hillside. The trail will lead you across the top of the hill heading north-west back towards the car park. The final section of trail is quite uneventful: after 1km you will pass over a forest access road and this puts you into the final section that leads back to the car park where you started the lap.

The entrance to the Black
option line

▶ALSO WORTH RIDING

ASHTON COURT – BRISTOL

Cross-country trails, Timberland trail 9km

Hotels and B&Bs in the area

Shops and cafes in Bristol city

Location: The trails are located in the parkland area behind the main gatehouse. They can be accessed from the Clifton Suspension bridge and are just off the main A369 Portishead road.

Grid ref: ST 558727

Sat nav: BS41 9NJ

Info: www.ashtoncourtestate.co.uk

GAWTON

Three Downhill tracks

HSD Red-grade trail, Egypt Black-grade trail and Super Tavi Black grade

Camping, hotels and B&Bs in the area

Uplift service available

Location: Heading north from Tavistock follow the A390 towards Gulworthy for approximately 22km (14 miles). Take a left turn onto the B3257 and follow for a couple of kilometres, you need to take a tight right turn into a narrow lane and head down towards the woodland, the car park is on the left.

Grid ref: SX 45859 69629

Sat nav: Tavistock

Info: www.woodlandriders.com

THE TRACK, PORTREATH

Jumps, pump track, slope style/freeride features

Campsite and cafe on site

Bike shop and bike hire on site

Location: Located near the Portreath Treasure Park, The Track can be found on the B330 off the main A30 Penzance trunk road. Follow the signs for Redruth and Treasure Park and The Track is on your right just after a crossroads.

Grid ref: SW 69047 44105

Sat nav: TR16 4HW

Info: www.the-track.co.uk

HAMSTERLEY

▶ FACILITIES

Car park and charges: Yes; charges apply

Cafe: Yes

Toilets: Yes

Showers: No

Bike wash: No

Nearest bike shop: On site

Bike hire: Yes

Accommodation: B&Bs in the nearby village and hotels in the surrounding area.

Other trails on site: Green, Blue, Red. Downhill tracks, jump lines and 4X track by permit. Permissive paths and forest roads.

Ordnance Survey map: Explorer OL31 and 305 for extra coverage to the east.

ENJOYMENT FOR SKILL LEVEL

Beginner: 7/10

Intermediate: 8/10

Advanced: 9/10

Getting there: Hamsterley forest is located to the west of Bishop Auckland just a few kilometres off the A68. Heading north on the A68 from Darlington (A1M) pass the turning (A688) to Bishop Auckland and continue for just over 7km to Witton Castle. Take the road on your left signposted to Hamsterley.

In the village centre, take a right turn heading north; you will see the signs for the forest and Toll Road on your left. The main car park is at the bottom of the hill by the forestry office.

Grid ref: NZ 09250 31191

Sat nav: DL13 3NL

More info: www.hamsterley-trailblazers. co.uk

▶ TRAIL 1

On-site grade: Black

Clive's grade: Red with Black sections

Distance: 12km

Technicality: 8/10

Ascent: 365m

ENJOYMENT FOR SKILL LEVEL

Beginner: 3/10

Intermediate: 7/10

Advanced: 8/10

Trailhead signage in the main car park

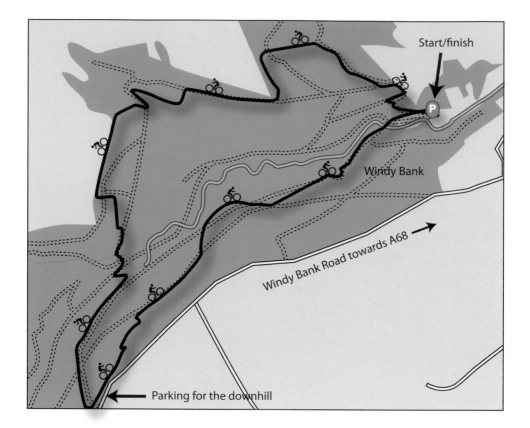

Tight rough single-track descents are a common theme

From the main car park at the visitor centre, roll along the forest road and bear right as you climb on a single-track trail. A right turn at the top puts you on a double track and within a few metres you turn left and continue to climb on single track up to a forest road.

The forest road climbs up out in open ground. After several hundred metres take a left turn into some single track. The trail continues to climb and the gradient is very mellow. Crest the hill-head straight on and start to descend.

The first descent is very rough and quite technical in places. The opening section of the descent runs parallel to a dry stone wall. If you get a chance to look over the top of this wall there are some lovely views out across the moorland to your right, however it is unlikely that you'll be able to take your eyes off the trail as large rocks protrude from the surface and many roots cast shadows and lure you in.

The lower part of the descent is quite steep and it's quite dark in the trees. There are also multiple lines to choose from as you weave your way down the hillside to join a forest road. This forest road links across to the next section of the descent down to a river crossing.

The trail leading you down to the river is very natural and fairly wide. There are multiple lines to choose from here and plenty of undulations in the surface to keep you entertained.

There is a footbridge to the left in case you don't fancy getting your feet wet in the ford. The trail beyond the stream climbs up and out and takes a right turn. You run parallel with the stream for a short distance before the trail bears left and starts to climb up out into open ground.

The next section of trail is named Route 666. This section climbs up the hillside in open ground, Here there are multiple desire lines, so make sure you turn in early and avoid the temptation to head straight on up a desire line. By doing so you get to traverse the hill out and make light work of the gradient.

The surface is very natural with root beds and rocks to add to the challenge. The upper part of the climb runs parallel to a dry

The ford may be deep in winter months and following periods of heavy rain. There is a bridge to the left if you don't fancy getting wet feet

stone wall and although the gradient isn't that steep the exposed root beds provide a good challenge and make for a technical climb. It is worth taking a moment to stop and look back at the views across the moorland.

Once you have crested the hill and start to descend, watch out for roots and wheel-grabbing holes as you drop down into the treeline – the low light levels here hide those rocks and roots. A short forest road link takes you to the next section, named Star Wars. This is very similar to the previous section with low light levels and plenty of

Dirt jumps and downhill tracks require top-notch skills and a permit

roots and rocks. At the end of this section take care as you drop out onto a country lane. Turn right and descend down the lane into a tight left-hand corner.

As you exit the corner you're presented with the option of going through a ford or you can take a footbridge to the left. After the stream crossing, join a forest road before turning left and climbing up a public road to the next forest road entrance on your right.

The next section will lead you up through the area where the downhill tracks run. Be aware that some of the tracks do cross over the climb, and riders may be approaching from your left at speed. Make sure you give way to these riders as they will have a much harder job in stopping the bike and slowing down.

Approximately halfway up the climb you will see a jump/skills area to your right. If you wish to ride any of these sections or areas you need to buy a permit which can be obtained in the car park at the top of this climb. When you arrive in the car park having completed your ascent bear left and pass through the car park into the Red downhill (at this point there were no signs for the Black trail).

This downhill really does get going and there are some option lines for you to choose, expect double jumps, tabletops, large berms, and hip jumps. A word of warning here: the hillside is relatively exposed and crosswinds can cause a problem when taking some of the jumps!

When you exit this jump line you have the option of taking a left to head back to the top for another run or following the main trail by taking a right turn. Traverse the hillside on this forest road for a short while before turning left and descending. This short single-track descent runs down to a narrow gully where the surface is loose, rough and slippery. Take care near the bottom of the section as you will drop down a large piece of rock and immediately into a wooden pinch fence before joining the public road.

You are now in the final stages of the trail. This public road will lead you uphill to the next section of single track. Join the single track on your left and start to descend once more. The gradient is relatively steep in places and there are jumps, roots, bomb holes and the inevitable rocks to deal with as you descend on a nice twisty trail. The trail links on to a forest road and once again you climb back up the hill before entering the final section of single track.

As you exit the final piece of single track join into a shared multi-user trail, this takes you back around to the forest drive and back to the car park.

There are a multitude of downhill trails at Hamsterley Forest, all of which are very technically challenging. To ride the downhill trails, jump spot, skills area and for cross track you need to buy a permit. These can be obtained from the car park mentioned above. The downhill runs are aimed at experienced riders only and are not suitable for novice riders. It may be worth taking a walk to have a look at the trails before you spend your money on a permit.

▶DOWNHILL TRAILS

Clive's grade: Orange/Black

Distance: N/A

Technicality: 8.5/10

ENJOYMENT FOR SKILL LEVEL

Beginner: 2/10

Intermediate: 6.5/10

Advanced: 8.5/10

There are many downhill tracks aimed at riders with a high level of experience

THE MARCHES – HOPTON WOODS

Orientate yourself on the map and read the information before heading out on the trail

▶ FACILITIES

Car park and charges: Yes; free

Cafe: No

Toilets: No

Showers: No

Bike wash: No

Nearest bike shop: Pearce Cycles, Fishmore Road, Fishmore, Ludlow, Shropshire SY8 3DP (01584 879288)

Bike hire: No

Accommodation: There are holiday homes, B&Bs, hotels and campsites in the area. Cavern Arms has the usual amenities.

Other trails on site: Blue route and taster loops, downhill tracks.

Ordnance Survey map: Explorer 201 & 217.

ENJOYMENT FOR SKILL LEVEL

Beginner: 3/10

Intermediate: 10/10

Advanced: 8/10

Getting there: Located on the Welsh border near Ludlow, Hopton Woods can be approached from all directions. From Ludlow, head west on the A4113, take the B4385 on your right just after Kinton and head north. Take a left then right through the village of Hoptonheath and just after the railway take a narrow lane on the left to Hopton Castle. Go through the village and climb uphill to the woods. The entrance is on your left and the car park is up the forest road beyond the fields.

Grid ref: SO 34811 77757

Sat nav: Hopton Castle, SY7 0QF

More info: www.forestry.gov.uk

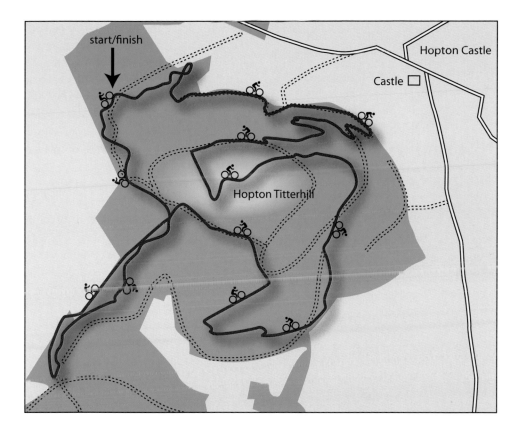

▶CROSS-COUNTRY TRAIL

On-site grade: Red

Clive's grade: Red with Black sections

Distance: 12km

Technicality: 8/10

Ascent: 440m

ENJOYMENT FOR SKILL LEVEL

Beginner: 3/10

Intermediate: 10/10

Advanced: 8-9/10

▶DOWNHILL TRAILS

Clive's grade: Orange/Black.

Distance: N/A.

Technicality: 8-9/10

DOWNHILLS: ENJOYMENT FOR SKILL LEVEL

Beginner: 3/10

Intermediate: 7/10

Advanced: 10/10

Pearce Cycles have contributed a huge amount to the trails here

The opening descent gives you a good idea of what lays ahead

Hopton is steeped in British mountain biking history: the hillside here has hosted national championships and regional competitions since the early 1990s. Local riders have ridden this hillside since the 1980s, so it was only time before the hard work paid dividends and an official marked trail was opened at the beginning of 2012.

One of few trails in the British Isles that begins with a downhill, the trail starts from the low side of the car park and twists its way through some tight trees. The lack of light in the trees makes visibility hard and on a wet day one can see it would be very slippery. At the bottom of the hill you cross a small ford and then run down the valley, crossing back over the stream before joining on to a forest road.

The forest road is fast and runs along the bottom of the hill before you take a tight right turn and climb up on single track. This section leads to the old quarry and has some steep gradients. It is worth thinking about the large climb further round the lap and conserve some energy here.

Crossing through the old quarry the trail becomes very rough. The last part of this section has some high-speed compressions, some of which have steep gradients leading you in and out. You rejoin the forest road and continue to traverse around the bottom of the hill with views to your left over towards the Castle.

The forest road turns and climbs up the hill, the gradient is quite steep and at the top of this section you will continue to climb in single track. The trail traverses the hillside out into the open and there's a steep ramp or two within this section. When you exit the single track however the climb heads up a steep forest break.

You will be surrounded by a good mix of deciduous and non-deciduous trees

Spectacular views of Shropshire

Climbing back up the steep hillside is split by terraced sections of single track

The trail now follows a forest road and continues to climb. The forest road is more of a break in the trees than a well-established gravel road, and you will end up crossing open ground with a knoll to your left. The trail runs around this knoll and it is from here that the majority of the downhill track starts from. You join in a trail that was once the original 1990s National Championships racecourse. As you can imagine, this is quite a technical descent: the speeds are high and the trail surface is natural and therefore rough. There are lots of roots, stumps and rocks to deal with and it's quite dark in the trees in the upper part of the trail too. When you break out off the trees the trail continues to pick up pace and you have to be on your guard not to let the large hits and speed get the better of you. You will turn right off the downhill track and into a built piece of trail and start to traverse the hill.

When you exit the single track you join on to a forest road at a switchback. The signage here can be confusing, just keep to the left-hand side of the switch and after a few metres of forest road the trail drops into a single-track section on your left. You pop out of the trees and traverse the hill – this section has recently been clear-felled and the trail swoops and snakes its way downwards across the hills.

A short section of forest road links you into a single track. This section is quite tight in the trees and there are plenty of natural features to keep it interesting. The climb is made up of two halves, you exit at the trees taking a left turn and traverse along a terrace. After a short rest and the chance to ease the legs you take a right turn and continue to climb up through a series of switchbacks. Here, once again, the trail feels very natural and some good skills will see you right when it comes to finding the flow.

The single track pops out onto a forest road and continues to climb up around the hillside. Signage is great and there are only a couple of junctions to deal with,

Swooping single track crossing clear-felled hillsides

and none of which should cause you any problems. The majority of the hard work is done now and there are some fun single-track sections and odd climbs to deal with before the loop is over.

The single track in the next section drops off to the left of the forest road. Here there are some tight switchbacks and some steep gradients, payback for all the climbing you've just done! Nearing the end of the section the trail levels out and you climb up through the trees. Take care at the end of this section as you drop out onto a forest road very close to a forest gate.

Just over the public road to your left is Bedstone Hill Car Park, where there are some fantastic views and this is also another place where you can park the car and start the ride. There is signage here giving route information and showing you where you

are on the trail. The trail itself takes a right turn from the last single track and climbs up the hillside through the trees. The trail joins an old 4x4 track and this section looks like it could become very wet and boggy on a winter's day. Continue to climb uphill into the trees before blending into a forest road. After a few metres the final section of single-track runs downhill back to the car park. There are some tight corners through this section and the trail surfaces are quite loose so take care.

There are a multitude of downhill trails at the Marches. They can be accessed from the main car park and are very well signposted. The downhill trails are very technical and it is essential to have the right sort of bicycles and equipment to safely partake of these trails. For more information and to download a map visit the forestry.gov.uk website.

RUSHMERE & OAKWOOD

The author takes a break from trails. The large chair is an obvious landmark at Rushmere

Rushmere is the new kid on the block. Having recently been acquired by the Green Sands Trust from a private landowner, mountain bike developments are new to this area of the forest. However, there has been a small mountain bike trail located to the north in Oakwood for quite a while. The new development at Rushmere links across to Oakwood via a network of permissive paths, including technical single-track trails. The area was formerly used as an arboretum so you will find a wide variety of species of deciduous and non-deciduous trees. This is another area where there is a network of natural trails and permissive paths, however we advise that you use only permissive bridleways and stick to the waymarked mountain bike trails.

▶FACILITIES

Car park and charges: Yes; charges apply

Cafe: Yes

Toilets: Yes

Showers: No

Bike wash: No

Nearest bike shop: Chaineys Cycles, Ropa Court, Friday Street, Leighton Buzzard, LU7 1DU (01525 852400)

Bike hire: No

Accommodation: B&B, hotels available in Leighton Buzzard and surrounding area.

Other trails on site: Blue family trail.

Ordnance Survey map: Explorer 192.

ENJOYMENT FOR SKILL LEVEL

Beginner: 7/10

Intermediate: 5/10

Advanced: 4/10

Permits: Permits are available form the ranger's office, located at nearby Stockgrove Country Park.

Getting there: The main entrance is located on the Old Linslade Road between Heath and Reach and Old Linslade. The entrance is on the northern side of the country lane and is well signposted.

Grid ref: SP 91207 28388

Sat nav: Old Linslade

More info: www.greensandtrust.org

▶TRAIL 1

On-site grade: Red

Clive's grade: Red with shared Blue sections

Distance: 7.5km

Technicality: 4/10

Ascent: 110m

ENJOYMENT FOR SKILL LEVEL

Beginner: 7/10

Intermediate: 6/10

Advanced: 4/10

From the main car park, located at the top of the hill opposite the bungalow, head northwards following the brown arrows with a bike logo located on plain wooden posts. As you exit the car park heading north you will turn right and then left through rhododendrons onto a main forest road. Continue for approximately 50m to the large chair and turn left, then keep left on a wider trail that runs alongside a dense plantation of young conifers.

You will enter a series of turns and cross over another path. After a few more metres you will cross a footpath. Just after the footpath there is a tight left-hand turn and the trail narrows. This section is slightly undulating and has a few blind corners. It should also be noted that this section is a two-way piece of trail, something that may change in the future. At the end of this section the trail takes a right turn into a gully and continues to run downhill. At

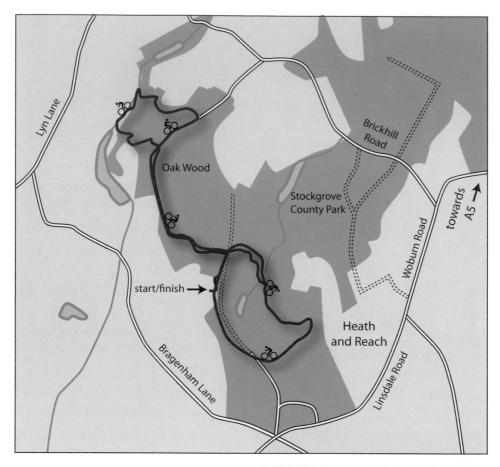

the end of the gully you will be faced with a tight right turn into a steep uphill bank. Climb up out of the gully where the trail then descends and is joined by a bridleway from the left. The visibility here is good so you should have no issues in spotting a horse and rider. The trail then joins into a junction with a footpath by a small pond. Be careful here as this is a busy part of the forest and you may come across other trail users.

Keeping the pond to your right, follow the main trail and head straight on up the bank in front of you (the main sandy bridleway will take a left turn at this point).

Brown arrows mark the route – make sure you get a permit before you ride

You traverse the hillside on a narrow piece of trail with the bridleway down to your left. At the end of this section join back on to the bridleway and continue climbing up for approximately 100m.

When you crest the hill you come to a crossroads. Take a left turn and climb up slightly, forking left as you do so. Pass over another wide trail into a tight single track. The trail at this point can become vague when there is a lack of foliage. The trail dips down slightly then bears hard right and climbs upwards with a fence and open ground to your right. You will then drop downhill slightly and continue to follow the forest boundary before a left-hand corner drops you into a small descent. Partway down the descent you will come to a forked junction: the left trail is just a shortcut that drops you onto the bridleway below, keep right at this point as the last section that traverses the hill is great fun.

At the end of the traverse the trail joins on to the bridleway so take care here as you switch hard left and climb back up on a wide hard-packed sandy trail. After approximately 30m take a tight right turn into a single-track section and traverse the hillside, this section of trail is part of the original Oakwood loop.

Be careful in the corners as the pine cones can roll under your tyres and the surface is quite loose in places. You will rejoin a bridleway, turning left as you climb upwards. Passing a footpath on your right, continue for a few more metres and turn right into the plantation and drop down a small hill with some tight turns before rejoining the main bridleway you climbed earlier on your outbound loop.

Pine cones litter the trails

The trail descends slightly and you need to fork left and retrace your steps, traversing the hillside on the single-track trail. Head back past the pond and climb up the steep bank before dropping into the galley and climbing uphill. You should recognise where you are at this point and the trail will take you back to the large chair. At this crossroads junction go straight ahead, keep left, then turn right through a gap in a fallen tree. A small climb leads you to a nice surprise section of trail.

The next section is a fantastic flowing downhill with bermed corners – 16 in total! The loose sandy surface may catch you out so take it easy on your first run, you can loop back up and repeat this section again if you wish to do so. When the descent enters the trees you will traverse the hillside down to a tight left-hand turn onto a double track where you turn right and then almost immediately left. Crossing through the bottom of the valley, you will be faced with a steep but short climb on the far side that heads up to your right. There are three trails at this point. The one up above you to your left is your return downhill trail for this section, the large wide trail to your right is for walkers, you need to stick to the centre trail and climb up. When you get to the top of this section, just to your right-hand side is a lookout offering a stunning view of the lake and the bungalow over by the car park from where you started. The mountain bike trail continues straight on at this point and you have the option of turning left and descending back down into the bottom of the valley.

If you add this extra loop you will get another chance to take on the 16 berms descent, and you will also get a short and steep descent back into the bottom of the valley. Take caution at the bottom of this section as you will be back at the multi-user junction. From the bottom of the valley cross over the small bridge and take a right turn. You will see the climb starts at the same point as the bottom of the descent and traverses its way around the hill. This climb feels very natural and is quite tough, although quite short. When you get to the end of this section of trail you will be back near the chair and you can take a switchback left into the 16 berms, head out for another lap of Oakwood or simply cycle back to the car.

Descend back through the 16 berms and retrace your steps through the valley and up the steep climb. When you exit the steep climb continue straight on along the double-track trail. Cross a footpath and continue straight on through the trees. At the end of this section turn right then left and be careful not to miss the next right turn (all these junctions are on top of each other). This final leg will take you to the lower car park near the gates where you entered. When you arrive in the grassy field continue straight over, crossing the main drive and up a double-track climb. This is a shared trail so be aware of other trail users. After a few metres of climbing there will be a trail on your right and this will lead you back to the main car park.

STAINBURN

▶FACILITIES

Car park and charges: Yes; free

Cafe: No

Toilets: No

Showers: No

Bike wash: No

Nearest bike shop: Chevin Cycles, Leeds Road, Otley, West Yorkshire LS21 1BR (01943 462773)

Bike hire: No

Accommodation: B&Bs, hotels and all amenities in nearby Harrogate and Otley.

Other trails on site: Black, various natural trails and permissive paths.

Ordnance Survey map: Explorer 297.

ENJOYMENT FOR SKILL LEVEL

Beginner: 3/10

Intermediate: 8/10

Advanced: 9/10

Getting there: From Otley: head north on the B6451 (there is a junction off to your left just outside Otley to continue on the B6451). You will pass a large reservoir. Climb up a steep hill and you'll find the car park at the top of the hill on your left. From the north: take the B6451 heading south from the A59 trunk road at Fewston. The car park will be on your right.

Grid ref: SE 20977 50857

Sat nav: Otley

More info: www.forestry.gov.uk

▶TRAIL 1: RED LOOP

On-site grade: Red

Clive's grade: Red

Distance: 1km

Technicality: 7/10

Ascent: 36m

ENJOYMENT FOR SKILL LEVEL

Beginner: 3/10

Intermediate: 9/10

Advanced: 7/10

Starting from the top right-hand corner of the car park the trail drops down to your right, the signage here for both the Red and the Black trails is quite vague. The opening section of the Red route is quite steep and you will have to negotiate a series of rocky and rooty drops. The trail then continues to twist its way down the hillside, and you'll have to negotiate some small rock gardens and loose corners.

Beyond the first descent the trail comes into the treeline and starts to climb back up the hill. The gradient is relatively easy and it's only a short climb before you

The Red and Black trails head out from the car park at the top of the hill

Rock and root drops on the Red will get you in the swing of things for the more challenging Black trail

switchback upon yourself and traverse across the hillside. You drop down slightly through more flowing turns. Here the trail surfaces are loose. A short rise sees you back at the car park with the opening part of the trail to your right.

▶TRAIL 2: WARREN BOULDER TRAIL

On-site grade: Black

Clive's grade: Black

Distance: 2.5km

Technicality: 10/10

Ascent: 110m

ENJOYMENT FOR SKILL LEVEL

Beginner: 0/10

Intermediate: 6/10

Advanced: 10/10

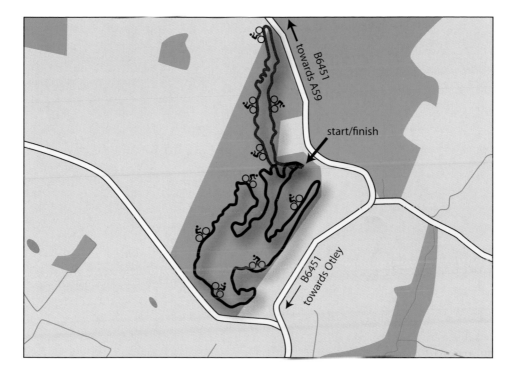

Starting in the same area as the Red trail, the Black trail passes over some stones set in the floor and forks off to the left. Within a few metres there is another fork in the trail and you need to take a left turn heading into the trees.

This trail really does live up to its grade and the opening section that traverses the hillside through the trees will give you a good indication of what lies ahead: roots, rock drops and steep gradients. After a few metres you will meet a split-line option with a technical drop to your right, alternatively you can go straight on turning right 90° into a rock slab. The exit to the slab is quite tricky as there are large rocks protruding from the trail bed for you to negotiate.

Rock slabs and bedrock on the Black trail

Painted logos on the trees will help you stay on track

From here the trail climbs back up the hillside. At the time of riding the floor was thick with pine needles and the ride line was quite vague. You will encounter multiple rock features as you start to descend back down the hillside. This is an exceptionally demanding trail. There are large rock outcrops and freestanding pieces of stone where the original trail ran, however, people have created desire lines around the majority of the main features.

While heading back down the hill there is the option of taking a boardwalk section. If you choose to do so you will be faced with a seesaw and a drop-off at the end.

The trail then turns back on itself and climbs back up the hill one more time. This short climb is followed by another short descent, which brings you out into the open at the bottom of the hill.

Climb up out in the open and once again the trail bed is littered with loose pieces of rock and large standing rocks. On the return climb you have the option of entering the trees once more or you can simply follow the main desire/push path trail back up to the top of the hill. This is clearly visible up ahead. If you do decide to go back into the trees once again you will find that the trail ride line is very vague, the signage is white squares with a pair of black dots that have been painted on the trees. Follow these for an extra loop that takes in some more challenging rocks and roots. The last section of the climb is quite steep and a good technical challenge.

►ALSO WORTH RIDING

KIELDER

Cross-country loops, 15km Deadwater trail and 2km Black Up and Over trail

Dead Water Downhill trail

Camping, hotels and B&Bs in the area

Bike shop, bike hire cafe and toilets on site

Location: Take the A7 from Carlisle heading north towards Hawick. Turn right at Cannonbie onto the B6357 signed for Newcastleton. Pass through Newcastleton and continue to the narrow bridge. Turn right after the bridge following the brown tourist signs to Kielder Water. Take a right turn onto the C200 and follow to Kielder village where you take a left turn signed to the forest and castle, take another left and climb up past the castle, car parking is up above the bike shop.

Grid ref: bike NY 62654 93526

Sat nav: Kielder Village

Info: www.forestry.gov.uk

LEE QUARRY

Cross-country trails, 5km Red trail and 1km Black loop

Hotels and B&Bs in the area

Facilities: Car parking on the roadside

Location: Located in the town of Bacup park near Futures Park and head up over the dirt bank and up the wide gravel trail. To get to Bacup, from the M60 leave at the M66 junction and head north. When the motorway ends follow signs for the A56 then take the A682 and A681 signed towards Bacup.

Grid ref: SD 866211

Sat nav: OL13 0BB

WHARNCLIFFE

Cross-country loop, Red 10km trail and various Downhill trails

Camping, hotels and B&Bs in the area

Location: From Sheffield pick up the A61 towards Barnsley, in Grenoside turn left onto Norfolk Hill and then turn right at the crossroads. Continue up the road to the woods and park in the first car park.

Grid ref: SK 325950

Sat nav: Grenoside.

Info: www.wharncliffe.info

THETFORD

▶ FACILITIES

Car park and charges: Yes; charges apply

Cafe: Yes

Toilets: Yes

Showers: No

Bike wash: Yes

Nearest bike shop: On site

Bike hire: Yes

Accommodation: B&Bs, hotels, self-catering accommodation and campsites in and around the forest area. Nearby Brandon and Thetford have all the usual amenities.

Other trails on site: Waymarked Green and Blue trails plus forest roads and permissive paths.

Ordnance Survey map: Explorer 229.

ENJOYMENT FOR SKILL LEVEL

Beginner: 10/10

Intermediate: 6/10

Advanced: 2/10

Getting there: The trails start at the High Lodge Forest Centre, the car park is up the forest drive just off the A1065 Mundford Road. Heading north out of Brandon stay on the main road for half a kilometre and you will see the flagpoles and gates on the right.

Post code: IP27 0AF

Grid ref: TL807864

Sat nav: Brandon

Info: www.forstry.gov.uk

Clear signage located near the main visitor centre

Thetford Forest has been home to mountain biking for many years. Back in the early 1990s a string of cross-country race events paved the way for the trail network to become a more official and permanent fixture. The trails themselves are made up from a mixture of fire breaks, forest roads and single tracks. The majority of the single-track sections were carved out for motorbike enduro events.

Created after the First World War and managed by The Forestry Commission Thetford is the largest lowland pine forest in the Britain. The forest covers a fair area and there are many trails cutting off here and there so you may want to take a map and go explore beyond the waymarked routes.

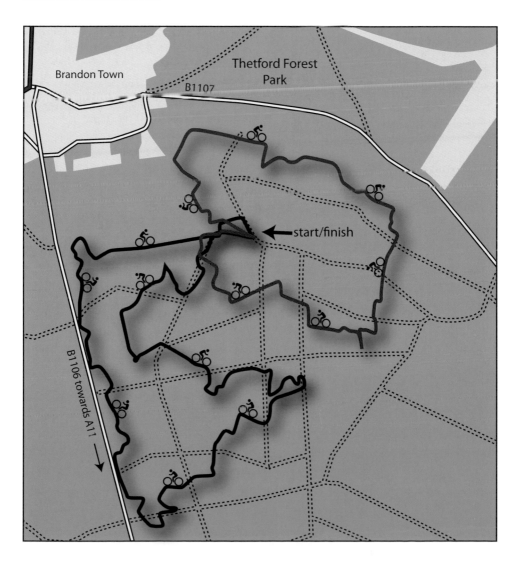

►TRAIL 1: BEATER TRAIL

On-site grade: Red – short version

Clive's grade: Blue with less than 10% Red sections

Distance. 10km

Technicality: 3/10

Ascent: 50m

ENJOYMENT FOR SKILL LEVEL

Beginner: 7/10

Intermediate: 5/10

Advanced: 3/10

Located in Norfolk it comes as no surprise that this trail is relatively flat. The Red trail comprises of flowing single track and open forest breaks. From the car park pick up the red posts with black arrows and head out over the forest drive before turning hard right at a four-way split crossroads. Take your time here as this section is two-way and it's easy to miss the tight right turn.

The trails are very well marked and it's hard to go wrong at any point. The Black trail will be straight in front of you after just a few hundred metres, bear right and keep following the red posts.

After a couple of kilometres you will cross the forest drive again and climb up a gentle incline by some telegraph poles. Another kilometre of easy-going hard-pack trail and you turn left into a plantation. Here

Forest breaks link single-track sections

the trail leads you through the trees with some fun flowing turns before you pop out onto another break.

Once again you will cross the forest road after approximately 5.5km from the start. Shortly after the trail hits the tight single track again, there is a split-line option, the left line has some nice banked turns and the right option cuts a straight line down through the trees. This is all well surfaced and easy-going stuff.

At 6.5km in the trail splits, you can opt out and ride the shorter loop by going straight on or take the left turn for a longer option. The longer loop had a diversion in place when we rode here, which was a shame for at this point the trail became less manicured and felt more natural, and the root beds and wet bits made for fun riding. We rode the shorter version and decided to ride the Black marked trail as well (more on this later).

Choose your trail

On the signs at the split you may notice some marker pen additions informing you of the distance. Ignore these as they are not correct, according to our findings and GPS data. Another few kilometres of mixed trail and you come across a bomb hole, this is located just off the main line on the right as you exit a winding piece of single track. The hole is possibly the remains of the flint works that so radically changed this landscape long before trees were planted

Tight single track swoops through the trees

here, it could also have been created by a bomb dropped in the area through the Second World War, hence the mountain biker's name for such a trail feature. You'll find that the south of England is littered with these.

The remainder of the trail is similar in feel and flow. It is pretty uneventful for the experienced rider: other than the odd line choice and root to avoid it's not hugely challenging, however it is still quite physical as there is a tendency to want to go fast in order to get the buzz back and this can make some of the turns a little more challenging too. For the less-experienced rider it's a great starting place and the perfect trail.

▶TRAIL 2: LIME BURNER TRAIL

On-site grade: Black

Clive's grade: Red with less than 10% Black sections

Distance: 14km

Technicality: 3.5/10

Ascent: 74m

ENJOYMENT FOR SKILL LEVEL

Beginner: 7/10

Intermediate: 6/10

Advanced: 4/10

The Lime Burner trail heads out from the visitor centre along the same route as the Red trail. Where the Red branches right continue straight on between the two

You will see further signage where the trail splits off

large black signs and follow the trail ahead – you're looking for black posts with a yellow tile and black arrow. The trail is very similar in feel to the Red for the first few kilometres, winding its way along forest breaks between the trees.

The first section of single track you get to has a few split-line options. Be careful not to stray off the main trail (marked by those black posts) as you could end up on one of many non-waymarked trails that Thetford has to offer. The best option if the trail direction becomes vague is to keep going straight on and look for the obvious evidence of bikes. On a wet day I should imagine the trail to be quite hard on equipment, the soil is quite sandy and the Black trail has not been surfaced like the Red, the fine silica deposits will reap havoc on drive and stopping components.

The day I rode the trail there was still quite a lot of moisture in the surface and this meant that some sections were quite tacky, so although the loop is relatively flat it will still burn some calories. I had ridden Thetford before so I knew what to expect and was sparing with the chain lube and energy expenditure.

The trail passes through young plantations

At the furthest point on the trail you start heading north on the return leg. The trail runs next to the B1106 and winds its way gently downhill for a while. After you cross a forest road near Mayday Farm you enter a section named 'The Beast': this section of trail is a lot of fun, small dips and blind crest with flowing turns wind downhill.

The elevation loss here is minimal at 30m but the trail dips in and out of natural hollows and some of the gradients are steep enough that keeping up speed is no issue, but be careful on the blind crests as the trails often turn just as you go over the top.

After another forest road crossing, head back up through some old deciduous trees and you're only a few kilometres away from the end. The final stretch is plain sailing and a wide sandy forest track leads you up next to an open field at Lingheath Farm and back to the High Cross visitor centre.

WHINLATTER

►FACILITIES

Car park and charges: Yes; charges apply

Cafe: Yes

Toilets: Yes

Showers: No

Bike wash: Yes

Nearest bike shop: On site

Bike hire: Yes

Accommodation: B&Bs, hotels, camping in and around the area, all amenities in nearby Keswick.

Other trails on site: Blue, skills loop, permissive paths and forest roads.

Ordnance Survey map: Explorer OL4.

ENJOYMENT FOR SKILL LEVEL

Beginner: 5/10

Intermediate: 8/10

Advanced: 8/10

Getting there: From the M6 at Penrith head west towards Keswick on the A66, go past Keswick and take a left turn at Braithwaite village following the signs to Whinlatter. The car park entrance is at the top of the steep hill on your right.

Grid ref: NY 20970 24591

Sat nav: CA12 5TW

More info: www.forestry.gov.uk

►TRAIL 1: ALTURA TRAIL NORTH & SOUTH LOOPS

On-site grade: Red

Clive's grade: Red

Distance: 19km

Technicality: 6/10

Ascent: 485m

ENJOYMENT FOR SKILL LEVEL

Beginner: 4/10

Intermediate: 8/10

Advanced: 7/10

The trail starts from the top end of the car park up near the bike shop. Throughout the opening section of single track you will have a couple of Black-option lines to your left – be careful if you do take these option lines as the first one has a steep rock drop back onto the main Red trail and the second option line has a boardwalk that drops you back onto the trail. If you're riding with a friend or in a group they may want to slow and give you room to drop back in.

The single track joins on to a forest road and after a few metres switching round the gully you branch off to the right and descend on more single track. You may find that the surface here is quite loose so take it easy and get used to the grip available – there will be plenty more downhill corners

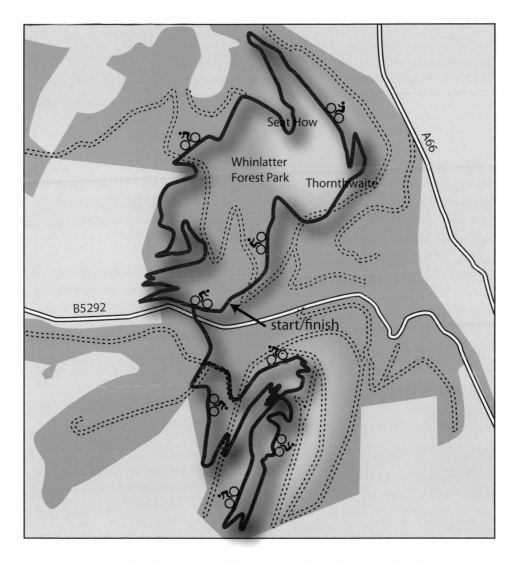

in the latter stages of the loop. The trail also climbs for some considerable distance so it is worth conserving some energy through these early single-track sections.

As you make your way up the hillside you will have some absolutely stunning views back out across the fells. The gradient is quite steep in certain places and you will have some tight switchback turns to negotiate as you traverse the hillside. The

trail joins a forest road and continues to climb. When you reach the top of this forest road section you will turn left and start traversing across the hilltop, climbing up through more switchbacks.

You will then start your traverse on a section of single track, the trail descends slightly before joining a short climb on a forest road linking you to the next downhill section. The downhill is relatively long and you will find rock drops, loose surface, berms and the odd jump. Some sections of the descent are quite steep and some of the corners tighten up on themselves, and the shale surface is loose and slippery in places.

At the bottom of the descent you come out onto the road near the entrance to the car park. To ride the south loop cross over the country lane through the pinch fence and follow the wide path down to a forest road. All the trails here are very well signposted so you should have no issues in navigating your way round.

The forest road continues for just a couple of kilometres before you peel off into a single-track section and a short climb links you to yet another forest road. Join the forest road, take a switchback to the right and continue to climb up. You'll be at the base of a large hill to your left and this is where you are heading up.

At the end of the forest road a single-track trail berms left and starts to climb up the hillside. Once again the climb is quite long so take your time and enjoy the stunning views back across to Whinlatter forest.

Throughout the climb you will encounter root and rock steps as well as the familiar tight switchbacks: this side of the trail is far more exposed than the other and would probably be best avoided on severe weather days.

Partway up the climb you will join on to another forest road. Here the descent crosses over in front of you so if you needed to take a shortcut, simply head straight on and drop in to the left. To continue on the main trail you need to take a switchback and follow the double track/forest road. The junction is quite confusing and the signs almost indicate that you should join the single track just above you – if you try to do so you will hopefully see the no entry signs.

Following the double track/forest road, continue to climb around the hillside and link to another single-track section of

The bench cut trail has a loose surface and speeds are quite high here

The small bridge signifies the start of the climb

climb. Once you arrive at the top of the hill you have a few rocky outcrops to deal with and it's worth pausing to enjoy the stunning views. The trail crosses the top of the hill, then drops down and climbs up to another cairn. At this point you start to descend and once again the surface is quite loose with the corners offering support on the entrance but not the exit!

Top: Looking back across to the north loop
Right: Rock crag at the top of the south loop

Drops and jumps in the final descent

A series of wide-open corners and rock drops with occasional jumps thrown in for good measure lead you back down to the crossing point that you passed earlier on in the climb. Cross over the double track and drop into another section of single track. Take care as this hillside is very exposed and on windy days jumping may be a problem. There is also a split-line option during this descent, the Black option is a wooden boardwalk and drop off to which there is no real landing ramp, so if you decide to take this prepare yourself as you will have to work hard to absorb the landing.

Throughout the lower sections you will cross over some forest roads and drop down some sections made from stone sets. There are also a few wooden pinch fences for you to pass between, which will slow you down as you cross over other trails.

When you arrive at the bottom of the descent, join a forest track and turn left climbing back up to where you headed on your outbound loop. Take a right turn here and return on the shared trail back to the country lane and the main entrance to Whinlatter Forest.

WOBURN

▶ FACILITIES

Car park and charges: Yes; free

Cafe: No

Toilets: No

Showers: No

Bike wash: No

Nearest bike shop: Chaineys Cycles, 15 Benbow Court, Shenley Church End, Milton Keynes, MK5 6JG (01908 504004)

Roy Pink Cycles, 19 St Johns Street, Newport Pagnell, MK16 8HE (01908 210688)

Phil Corley Cycles, Unit 3, Stacey Bushes, Milton Keynes MK12 6HS (01908 311424)

Bike hire: No

Accommodation: B&Bs, hotels in Woburn Sands and Woburn.

Other trails on site: There are lots of permissive paths on the estate but you will need to buy an annual or day permit from the ranger's office at Stockgrove Country Park near Leighton Buzzard.

Ordnance Survey map: Explorer 192.

ENJOYMENT FOR SKILL LEVEL

Beginner: 8/10

Intermediate: 7/10

Advanced: 5.5/10

Permits: You can get a permit at the ranger's office located at Stockgrove Country Park, Brickhill Road, Heath & Reach, Leighton Buzzard, LU7 0BA.

A pass will cost £10.00 per annum. This can also be purchased from the warden and you can also pay for a day ticket.

Getting there: Woburn Woods are located just on the outskirts of Woburn Sands village near Milton Keynes in Buckinghamshire. The Woburn estate, owned by the Duke of Bedford, forms part of the Greensands Ridge that runs from Leighton Buzzard to Gamlingay. The woods can be accessed from many different places. For the jumps and drops park up in the layby just outside Woburn Sands as you head south on the A5130 towards Woburn village, the layby is on your right as you crest the hill. There is more parking at the top of Church Road, which is accessible from the mini roundabouts at the south end of Woburn Sands high street. The village has a well-stocked store, banks and a petrol station. There are also various pubs and restaurants located in the area.

Grid ref: SP 90749 34547

Sat nav: Woburn Sands

More info: www.greensandtrust.org

77

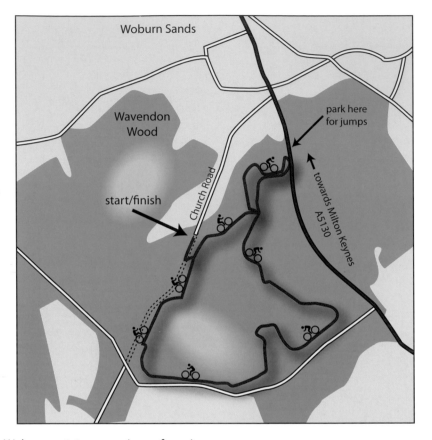

The Woburn estate comprises of a pine plantation mixed with deciduous trees; the area where you will be riding your bike is mainly made up from a mixture of pines. The estate is managed by Bedford Estates and the Green Sands trust; access to the land has been granted by the Duke of Bedford by permit only. There are many trails in this area. The woods are split into differently named plots. The most popular area of the wood is located to the south of the church in Apsley Heath. The jump area is situated just north of Old Wavendon Heath, opposite the disused quarry.

You will need an Ordnance Survey map to navigate on permissive paths, bridle-ways, public roads and access tracks.

Don't let the poor signage deter you from one of the best UK jump spots

Development for mountain biking continues across the estate and you can now link to the Rushmere estate via public roads through Little Brickhill, taking you onto the south side of Watling Street (the A5).

▶ TRAIL 1

On-site grade: No grade is given by the estate owners

Clive's grade: XC Blue with Red sections

Distance: Various; 7.5km

Technicality – XC: 3/10

Technicality – jumps: 7–10/10

Ascent: 120m

ENJOYMENT FOR SKILL LEVEL

Beginner: 8/10

Intermediate: 6/10

Advanced: 5/10

Park at the top of Church Road and ride through the car park until you reach a pair of gates on opposite sides of Sandy Lane. Go through the gate on the left and continue along the sandy gallops for a few metres before turning left down a double track. Follow this to the end, bearing right, and continue along a hard-packed smooth track to a fork where you bear left. Keep to the main sandy track as this bears round to the right slightly and at the next crossroads take a right turn. (If you want to head to the jumps at this point, you should continue straight on and the trail will bear left. This single-track trail continues for 100m, where you take a tight right turn before dropping down onto a wider track that runs around the top of the jump area.)

Our short 7.5km cross-country loop continues right from this junction and follows a fence and a bank to your left. At the end of this section, veer left onto the main sandy trail and continue along the gallops for a couple of hundred metres. Just before the gallops start to drop-down you will notice the plantation of large pines on your right ends. Here you drop down a steep sandy bank onto a main trail below. This section is good fun, the gradient is quite steep and will keep even an experienced rider on their toes. At the bottom of this steep bank bear right onto a hard pack double track and continue to climb upwards around the hillside. You will come to a fork where you need to turn left and after a few metres join another trail where you turn left again. Up to your right you will notice a single-track trail. This is specifically for bikes and can be ridden in either direction. Personally I prefer riding this in the opposite direction but for the purposes of this loop we joined the single-track trail and traversed the hillside.

Cross over a couple of bridleways and, as always, take care when doing so! The trail will lead you down to a car park and picnic area. Having passed through the Old Wavendon Heath you will now climb up slightly through New Wavendon Heath and back to the Sandy Lane. The Sandy Lane will be on your left-hand side as you continue to climb upwards, although the hills are small you can link up trails up to make quite a tough ride with a reasonable amount of climbing. At the top of this section you will join a sandy bridleway, take

Sandy single track with jumps and drops are all over the woods

a left turn to take you back to Sandy Lane. There are so many trails in this area you can ride for many hours and not cover the same trail twice, however it should be noted that not all the trails in the area are on your Ordnance Survey map and not all the trails are permissive routes for a bicycle. This short loop will give you a taste of what's out there. I highly recommend spending some time in this area discovering the many fun, flowing single-track trails. I used to ride here as a child and Back Wood over near the golf course was a particular favourite spot. There are many riders in the area who would be willing to show you around, just take a look on the Internet.

▶JUMP PARK AND DOWNHILLS

Clive's grade: Jumps and downhills – Orange/Black

Distance: N/A

Technicality – jumps: 6–10/10

Technicality – downhills: 6.5/10

JUMPS: ENJOYMENT FOR SKILL LEVEL

Beginner: 2/10

Intermediate: 7/10

Advanced: 10/10

DOWNHILLS: ENJOYMENT FOR SKILL LEVEL

Beginner: 7/10

Intermediate: 6/10

Advanced: 5/10

The jump area has been developed over several years. Here you will find various downhill lines, dirt jump lines, and technical trails to test your skill. The start of the downhill runs are located on the boundary trail which you can access via the directions above. If you enter the jump area from the lower corner and main road that runs between Woburn Sands and Woburn you will need to push up the main double track to the left of the jumps to access the start of the DH runs. From the top of the hill you can take trails to your right that run around the boundary to the entrance gate, or you can take trails that run along the ridgeline above the jumps and break either right into the main jump area or left into a secondary jump area. This is a very popular spot and you should take care when crossing trails as there may be other riders crossing your path. The main push-up path is also a designated bridleway and footpath so you should be aware of other forest users when crossing or using this trail to access the downhill tracks.

WALES

AFAN FOREST PARK

▶ FACILITIES

Car park and charges: Yes; charges apply

Cafe: Yes at both centres

Toilets: Yes at both centres

Showers: Yes at both centres

Bike wash: Yes at both centres

Nearest bike shop: On site at Glyncorrwg and Afan Forest Park

Bike hire: Yes

Accommodation: Camping sites are available on site at Glyncorrwg. There are also plenty of B&Bs in the area catering for the mountain bike trade. Cymmer is located halfway between the two centres and is a handy place to base yourself. Another good location is Bryn Bettws log cabins located at the top of the Wall trail.

Other trails on site: Skyline, long Red/Black-graded trail, forest roads and permissive paths.

Ordnance Survey map: Explorer 166.

ENJOYMENT FOR SKILL LEVEL

Beginner: 4/10

Intermediate: 9/10

Advanced: 8–9/10

Getting there: From the M4 junction 40 head north and turn left at the mini roundabout onto the A4107 following the brown signs to Afan Forest Park. After approximately 7km, Afan car park is on your right. For the Glyncorrwg visitor centre continue further up the main road to Cymmer and turn left following the signs to Glyncorrwg. The centre and car parks are on your left just before the village.

AFAN

Grid ref: SS 82147 95124

Sat nav: SA13 3HG

GLYNCORRWG

Grid ref: SS 872000 98464

Sat nav: SA13 3HG

More info: www.afanforestpark.co.uk

▶ TRAIL 1: THE WALL

On-site grade: Red (Black when linked as W2)

Clive's grade: Red

Distance: approximately 24km (40km when linked to Whites level)

Technicality: 6–7/10

Ascent: 919m (W2 Trail)

ENJOYMENT FOR SKILL LEVEL

Beginner: 4/10

Intermediate: 8/10

Advanced: 7/10

Trail signage

From the Afan car park head up by the visitor centre and join the trailhead. The trail traverses across the hillside, dips down and goes through a bridge underneath the road. Turn left into a piece of single track named Alpha. At the end of this section take a tight right-hand switch and run down the double track to another single-track trail on your left. This will be the first pinch gate of many you encounter around the Afan Forest. Just beyond the gate the trail drops down some stone sets and into a series of concrete berms.

Exit through another pinch gate and cross the river. You will start to climb uphill as you bear right in an eastward direction with the river down to your right. At this stage you're on a double track.

Take a single-track trail (The Elevator) on your left and traverse the hill. At the

Concrete berms drop you down to the river

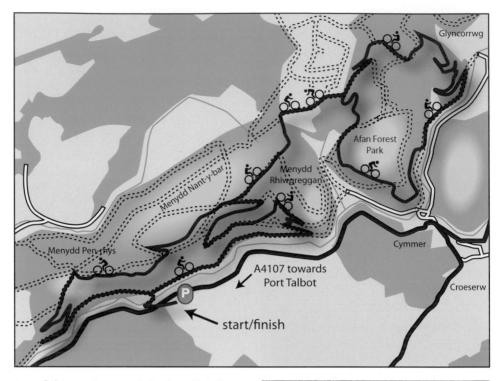

top of this section you join the old railway and continue running eastwards with the river to your right in the valley below. In just over a kilometre the trail switches left and climbs up a forest road. Here there are some spectacular views back down the valley. A further kilometre of climbing and the trail turns right into a single track and continues to climb.

You will come into a clear-felled section before exiting the single track onto a forest road. Climb for a few hundred metres and a single-track trail will veer off on your left. The following section of single track will come out into the open as you come around the front of the hill and start to descend. It is a fantastic section of trail

*Fresh bench cut trail
climbs the steep hillside*

but be aware: partway down there is yet another pinch gate!

After the gate the single track drops onto a forest road, which continues to climb for approximately 1km. After a left-hand switch on the forest road a single-track trail heads off on your right. Switch right into this trail traversing the hillside once again. The gradient here is minimal and is a fun flowing section of trail.

A short forest road section links you to a single track, which will eventually rejoin the forest road. At the top of the climb you have the option of turning left to continue on The Wall trail, or to turn right to head outbound and link up with Whites Level.

After just over 1km the forest road takes a right-hand turn. At this point head straight on into a break in the trees. This section can become quite wet and boggy. It is also a shared trail so be aware of oncoming traffic!

Nearing the end of this section the ground becomes particularly wet. Lines change often here and the left line may be eroded by the time you get there. If you stay high on the left you can ride the bank above the boggy ground and it's a fun challenge to navigate your way through

Forest road climbs link sweet single tracks

this section and not put a foot down. Exit the trees and turn left onto a forest road. Here you start to drop down with the wind turbines in the distance over to your right.

At the bottom of the descent you will come to a right turn through a gate and over a cattle grid. Continue traversing the hillside on open ground following the forest road past the wind turbines up to your left. From the cattle grid it's approximately 1.5km until you reach the single-track trail of Whites Level, you will see trail on the left and trail dropping down on your right.

▶ TRAIL 2: WHITES LEVEL

On-site grade: Red, Black when linked as W2

Clive's grade: Red

Distance: approximately 15km (40km when linked to The Wall)

Technicality: 7/10

Ascent: 919m (W2 Trail)

ENJOYMENT FOR SKILL LEVEL

Beginner: 3/10

Intermediate: 7/10

Advanced: 7–8/10

Switch right into a section of single track that has been named Energy and instantly you're presented with a series of tabletops and large whoops. You will also encounter some rocky drops and blind crests throughout this section; there is a narrow boardwalk to deal with too. After the boardwalk the trail traverses the hillside out

in the open; the surface is heavily eroded at this point and quite rough. Nearing the end of this section you will twist round into a gully. The trail tightens down here and there are some good rocks and routes to deal with.

On the opposite side of the gully a switchback climb leads you up the hill into the trees. At the top of this section exit through the pinch gates onto a forest road. Climb up for a few metres on the forest road. Bear round to the right and into the next section of single track, this trail is named Goodwood. The trail traverses the hillside and has some fast sections, there is also the option of taking a boardwalk and this is highly advisable on wet days as the alternative trail becomes quite soft. The boardwalk crosses over the single track so just be aware of other riders approaching

Snaking single track on the recent clear-felled hillside

Glyncorrwg visitor centre

from your left – the two lines eventually blend back into one trail. At the end of this section join a forest road, continuing straight on climbing up slightly before turning off the forest road right into another section of single track.

The trail starts to descend round the hill front and the Glyncorrwg Valley will be down on your right-hand side. There are some option lines in this section where you can take larger rocky drops. There are also quite a few blind crests, drop offs and fast whoops to deal with. The trail opens out in front of you, snaking its way downwards across the hillside. You enter an outcrop of trees in the lower section where you come into a tight right-hand switchback. After this there are more option lines for large rock drops. A tight left switch and the final few metres descend before the trails joins the tarmac cycleway.

Turn left onto the cycleway and continue

northwards with the river down to your right. After a kilometre you will see a single track on your left, this is the start of the Whites Level trail. If you want to take a break you can continue north back to the Glyncorrwg visitor centre – simply follow the signs.

Turning left you start another large climb. There are some loose steep sections and wet sections, and the climb blends into a double track where you traverse round the hill before taking a left switchback climbing on a double track. This steep section only lasts a few metres and you turn tight right into more single track. The single-track trail will eventually join into another forest road. Climb up a few more metres on the forest road before the trail bears right, the gradient increases and the surface becomes very loose. Pass another gate into the next section named Dastardly and Mutley.

The upper section of the climb is called Two Tombs. This section will lead you to a wooden pinch gate where there is the option line to take a Black-grade trail on your left. If you do decide to take the Black trail you will encounter some rocky sections, steep gradients and jumps. The forest road at the bottom of this trail leads you back up the hill to the main junction where you can rejoin the Whites Level trail. The main trail continues straight on through the pinch gates, blending into a forest road when there is a crossroads. Head straight across and up to your right onto a narrow forest road before taking a left fork into another piece of single track. The wind turbines will be up in front of you above the treeline and you will go through another pinch gate into this section, which has been named Windy Point. The section traverses around the hillside and the gradient starts to dip down, there are some nice fast shallow turns that will lead you through and out of

The return leg on W2 linking into windy point

the trees into a rough section before taking a left-hand switchback, dropping down the hillside and continuing back into the treeline. At the end of this section you will come to a pinch gate and a tight turn onto a forest road, this is where you started the White Level loop.

If you wish to continue on the Whites Level trail drop in for your second lap or alternatively turn right on the forest road and retrace your steps back across to The Wall.

Having followed your steps back to the forest road junction with The Wall continue left and then right across the forest road. The trail is well signposted but do take your time as this is quite a fast section. You will join another section of single track and the trail starts to traverse the hillside, this section is fast and the surface is quite loose and rough at times.

There will be a few sections over the next couple of kilometres that climb up ever so slightly. The final section of trail becomes exceptionally fast in places and there are also some tight whoops and blind crests to deal with, so be careful not to let the bike run away from you.

At the time of writing there was some diversions in place as a new single-track section was being built to lead you back down to the river. We traversed along the forest road before entering a newly built piece of single track to our right. This switched back downhill and dropped us onto the disused railway where we ran parallel to the river in a westerly direction back to the bridge. After crossing the river there is a final sting in the tail as you climb back up underneath the road and up to the visitor centre.

BETWS-Y-COED – GWYDYR FOREST

▶ FACILITIES

Car park and charges: Yes; charges apply

Cafe: No

Toilets: No

Showers: No

Bike wash: No

Nearest bike shop: Tan Lan/Holyhead Rd, Betws-y-Coed, LL24 0AB (01690 710766)

Bike hire: From above shop, nothing available on site

Accommodation: B&Bs, hotels, camping and all amenities in nearby Llanrwst and Betws-y-Coed.

Other trails on site: Natural trails/permissive paths and forest tracks.

Ordnance Survey map: Explorer OL17.

ENJOYMENT FOR SKILL LEVEL

Beginner: 3/10

Intermediate: 9/10

Advanced: 8–9/10

Getting there: From the A5 just south of Betws-y-Coed (before the metal bridge) take the A470 heading north to Llanrwst. After the railway bridge, take a left turn over a narrow stone bridge. At the end of the strait the main road bears right and you need to take a left turn (signed for Betws-y-Coed) then immediately turn right up a steep narrow lane. The car park is on your left at the top of the hill.

Grid ref: SH 79028 60948

Sat nav: LL26 0PN

More info: www.mbwales.com

▶ MARIN TRAIL

On-site grade: Red

Clive's grade: Red

Distance: 25km

Technicality: 7/10

Ascent: 680m

ENJOYMENT FOR SKILL LEVEL

Beginner: 3/10

Intermediate: 9/10

Advanced: 8–9/10

Trail signage

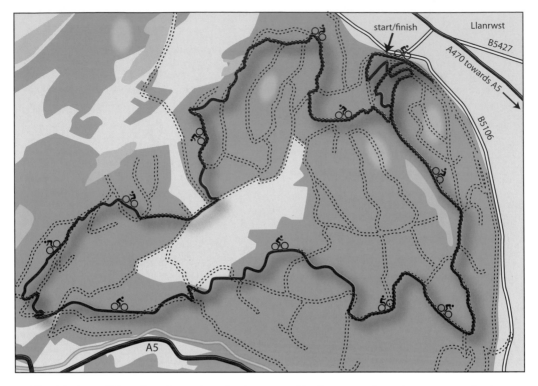

The Marin trail is a firm favourite of mine for many reasons. For me, it encompasses a good spoonful of all the essential ingredients that make for a great ride: flowing single track to fast forest roads, tough climbs to mellow gradients, stunning views to tight trails twisting through the trees. It's just a shame there are no on-site facilities to back up this challenging Red-grade loop.

The trail heads out from the high side of the car park and starts with a single-track climb. This is the start of quite a long climb and can be a shock to the system if you're not warmed up. The single track joins a forest road where you take a right turn and continue to climb. You will pass over a crossroads and continue straight ahead. Remember this spot as this is where you will cross over on your return leg.

The forest road continues across the top of the hill for a short distance before you take a right turn into a single-track section. The single track descends and crosses over another forest road taking a right/left turn, the next section is quite steep in places and the surface is loose and rough.

At the end of this section take a left turn and cut across another forest road before entering the final piece single track in this descent. The last section pops you out onto yet another forest road where you take a left turn. The forest road cuts around the bottom of the hill before taking a left turn and climbing up onto a public road, a right turn into the car park by the old mine workings links to a climb up another forest road.

Nearing the top of the hill the trail turns right and you're into a wonderful flowing

The first descent is full of fun features

The loose surface requires respect

piece of single track. At the end of the section you will blend onto another forest road by taking a left turn and climbing up slightly. Then a short single-track section leads on to another forest road. Here on a clear day you have spectacular views across to your right with the mountains of the Snowdon range in the distance.

Take a right turn at a T-junction then left into another section of single track. This section of trail is quite rough and there are some interesting technical features. At the

end of the section, take a left turn onto a forest road before another downhill section of single track links to a junction with a public road. Here you have the option of taking a left turn to cut back to the car park should you have any problems. The main trail takes the right turn and runs down the public road for a few hundred metres passing open ground on your right.

The old mines at the start of the second climb

Take a right turn off the public road onto a forest road climb; it's only a short climb and the gradient is fairly easy. The forest road descends slightly before you take a left turn and climb up on a single track. A short descent drops you onto yet another forest road, this is a short link, which leads you down to the section known as the Dragon's Tail.

Dragon's Tail is a nice flowing piece of single track. Partway through this section you will cross a small bridge and take a hard right turn climbing up some steps. The following section of trail is named Pixie's Paradise, and it will run you back down to the public road.

Cross over the road and follow the

A tough technical challenge, these rock steps can be ridden but you will spend some serious energy in the process

forest road descending and climbing. This section of forest road is very fast and the long downhill helps make light work out of the climb. It's a great opportunity to carry some speed into the climb – my Garmin GPS unit informed me I'd hit 54km/h on this descent! This gives you some idea how much speed you can carry into the following climb.

As you crest the climb on the forest road take a left turn and you are presented with a very steep climb on a public road. After a couple of hundred metres you take a single-track trail on your right-hand side. The trail continues to climb, traversing across the top of the hills. The following section, 'Stump Dance', runs on for some considerable distance and links to another forest road that traverses around the hillside.

A sweet technical section of single track will pop you out at the end of the lake. You have a nice easy flat section of forest road leading past the lake. This is a chance to enjoy the view and catch a breath because you will go straight on at a crossroads and climb a steep gradient on a double track. The trail crosses the hilltop before a short descent leads you into a single-track climb where you will cross over the forest road you took on your outbound trail.

You are now at the top of the final descent. A long flowing section of single track leads you back down to the car park. The final descent has some nice corners, jumps, whoops and many blind crests to deal with. You really do get a good reward for all the forest road miles you've covered. At the bottom, take a tight switchback into the overflow car park, run down the public road before turning off right and traversing the hill on the final single track.

BRECHFA

▶ FACILITIES

Car park and charges: Yes; charges apply

Cafe: No

Toilets: Yes

Showers: No

Bike wash: No

Nearest bike shop: Steve's cycle centre, New Road, Ceredigion, SA44 1QJ (01559 363653 or 07866 534966)

Bike hire: No

Accommodation: B&Bs in Brechfa village, hotels, self-catering accommodation and campsites further afield.

Other trails on site: Green, Blue, Red, forest roads and permissive paths.

Ordnance Survey map: Explorer 186.

ENJOYMENT FOR SKILL LEVEL

Beginner: 7/10

Intermediate: 9/10

Advanced: 8/10

Getting there: From Carmarthen take the A40 heading east towards Llandello. At Nantgaredig turn left onto the B4310, follow the road through Brechfa village for 1.5km. The car park for the Blue, Green and Black trails is on your left. Alternatively, continue along the main road and park further up in the village of Gorlech for the Red trail.

Grid ref: SN 54485 31576

Sat nav: Brechfa

More info: www.mbwales.com

Brechfa forest has gone from being a royal hunting ground to a mountain biker's trail hunting ground. The forest was instrumental in the Industrial Revolution of South Wales and timber was harvested here in the First World War to help in the production of explosives. The forest is currently considered a multipurpose site and is used for timber production, recreation and wildlife conservation.

The small arrows can be hard to see, take care at junctions

▶RAVEN TRAIL

On-site grade: Black

Clive's grade: Black

Distance: 19km

Technicality: 7/10

Ascent: 618m

ENJOYMENT FOR SKILL LEVEL

Beginner: 2/10

Intermediate: 8/10

Advanced: 9/10

The trail starts at the high end of the car park. Climb up on the forest road for approximately 1km before turning left into single-track trail. The trail traverses around the hillside and is shared with the Blue and Green outbound trail. The surface is smooth and is relatively wide; it flows and swoops around the hillside dipping up and down slightly before you arrive to a split-line option. At a left-hand switchback the Black option line peels off to your right. The Black section consists of tight turns, rock drops, and jumps. On a wet day this section can become soft with boggy wheel-grabbing holes. The section concludes with a tight left-hand switchback after which there is

Smooth start to a fantastic trail

The skinny log ride at the bottom of the first descent

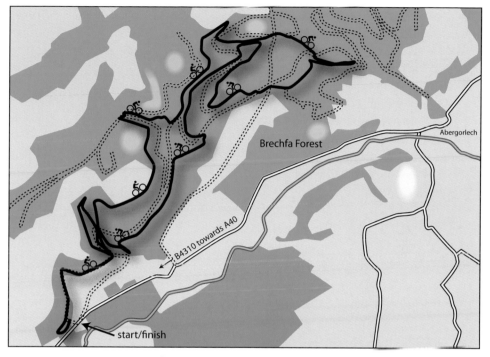

The map shows Brechfa Forest, with labels for Abergorlech, B4310 towards A40, and start/finish.

the option of a log ride before dropping onto a forest road where there is no sign. Take a right and head down the forest road, turn left and left again on the forest roads before starting the first proper climb.

You will climb up a steep gradient for approximately 300m, then switch right and continue to climb for another few hundred metres up through the treeline. This is a nice flowing section of single track, even though you're climbing. The trail dips down slightly as you traverse around the hill, but don't be fooled into thinking this is the descent as you will drop onto a wider track and start to climb up again.

At the top of this ramp there is a vague line in front of you, ignore this and branch right onto the larger more obvious trail. At the time of riding, the trail was still quite wet and one could imagine that it becomes hard work on a winter's day.

At the end of this section you start to descend. The gradient is quite steep, surface loose and the turns tight. You drop onto a forest road where you need to turn right before descending slightly (approximately 50m), branching off left into more single track. Exiting the single track, cross the forest road and here the trail flows down into the treeline where it gets progressively steeper. There is a series of large berms as you switch from either side of a gully snaking down the hill. The final stages of the single track have some lovely tight switchbacks, however, there were some soft patches that may catch you out if unawares. At the end of this section, you pop out onto a forest road. Take a left turn.

Following an old forest road, which is quite rough in places, you will have a gully to your left. This section continues to climb. The gradient is easy but take your time and save some energy because it's steep in its latter stages. At the top of the steep section you take a right turn into a section of single track and the trail continues to climb. You will know you're near the top when the trail starts to level out on a single-track cut in the grass. Through this section you will see an abandoned dry stone building to your left. The trail dips down slightly and has one last little steep section before joining a forest road.

The old stone building is a good indicator that you are near the top of the climb

Turn left then right on the forest road and continue to follow the signs to enter another piece of single track. This section is very fast in places but it does tighten up and become very narrow. The ride line opens up for its final section before joining the forest road where you take a right turn.

Traverse around the hillside with spectacular views out to your left. This section of forest road continues for a few kilometres. You will bear left at one junction before descending slightly and taking a junction to your right, climbing uphill. The forest road starts to descend, you will soon pick up speed but be careful for you need to take a single-track trail on your right. There are signs but at speed it's easy to miss.

The single-track trail traverses around the hill, descending and climbing ever so slightly. There is one section where you pass through a large dip in the trail. Be careful here: at the time of riding it was quite soft and wet in the bottom of this gully! Nearing the end of the section the trail starts to drop and the gradient gets quite steep. There are some more tight switchbacks to deal with before dropping onto a forest road and taking a right turn.

A shared trail descends and this is another fast section, the turns here offer little in the way of support and the surface is quite loose. Be careful not to get too 'lost in the moment' as the Black trail will take a left turn and climb up a steep bank. There are signs at this point but it's easy to miss them if you're focused on the trail ahead.

The following section climbs up slightly before descending into the jump line and skills area. This section opens with some tight switchbacks and some jumps before a small rock garden leads you into a line of

The large log bridge complete with handrails

tabletops. It's possible to ride or pushback up the forest road and loop this section up; if you choose to do so take a right turn at the bottom of the section joining the main forest road and simply follow the signs.

The Black trail continues straight down the gully and you really do get a sense of reward for your climb at this stage in the trail. At the bottom of the section you will cross over the river on a felled tree: don't panic, there are hand rails to keep you on track here. After the bridge, switchback up the gully side before descending on another fast section of single track. At the

end of the section there is an obligatory log ride which leads you on to a bridge. Crossing the bridge take a left turn and climb up out onto a forest road.

This forest road will bring you up to a left-hand turn, which you may recognise as this is where you headed outbound after the first small descent. The forest road brings you back around the front of the hill below the outbound trails and you will turn left into the final section of single track. This comprises of multiple blind crests and jumps and will come out just below the main car park.

CLI-MACHX – DYFI FOREST

▶ FACILITIES

Car park and charges: Yes; free

Cafe: No

Toilets: No

Showers: No

Bike wash: No

Nearest bike shop: The Holey Trail, 31 Heol Maengwyn, Machynlleth, SY20 8EB (01654 700411)

Bike hire: No

Accommodation: There are some B&Bs and a hotel nearby. There is also a campsite in Corris and lots more accommodation down the main road in Machynlleth.

Other trails on site: Permissive paths and forest roads.

Ordnance Survey map: Explorer 215 (plus OL 23 for extra coverage to the north and east).

ENJOYMENT FOR SKILL LEVEL

Beginner: 4/10

Intermediate: 9/10

Advanced: 7/10

Getting there: Located near the village of Corris 7km north of Machynlleth on the A4971, take the second turn to the village over the narrow bridge. The road

The donation box and trailhead signage

bears right then climbs uphill. At the fork, turn left and continue to climb up a narrow lane. The car park is located at the top of a forest road further up the lane on your left.

Grid ref: SH 76010 06379

Sat nav: Machynlleth

More info: www.mbwales.com

▶ CLI-MACHX TRAIL

On-site grade: Red (with the final descent being graded Black)

Clive's grade: Red

Distance: 15km

Technicality: 7/10

Ascent: 420m

ENJOYMENT FOR SKILL LEVEL

Beginner: 4/10

Intermediate: 9/10

Advanced: 7/10

The opening forest road climb is a tough one but you are rewarded with spectacular views

There is no doubt in my mind that most people would agree that this trail is all about the last descent, but that should not become the focus of the ride: the journey more often than not is more important (and enjoyable) than the destination itself.

On the flipside the ride starts with the serious business of climbing. The trail starts by continuing up on the forest road you drove in on, the gradient is relatively steep and the climb continues for a couple of kilometres so take your time, save energy and enjoy the spectacular views.

A few hundred metres past the second switchback the gradient levels out and you traverse the hillside heading towards your first section of single track. This section, however, is short-lived and you're back onto a forest road but only for a few metres before bearing right into single track. The gradient through here is pretty mellow

and you have to work hard to keep your momentum as you drop down the hillside to link onto another forest road.

This section of forest road only lasts for a few hundred metres and you'll be signed left to climb up a single-track trail and out into open ground. This section does descend slightly but will put you into yet another climb, so once again it's best to save some energy and if you get the chance to take your eye off the trail you can enjoy the spectacular views out to your right.

You will join an old double track and start climbing. At the top of this section you blend into a forest road. Make a mental note of this as you will return to this point after riding the far loop. Taking a right turn on the forest road, in a short distance you will see a pinch fence and single-track trail on your right. This section is relatively uneventful but that's not to say it doesn't

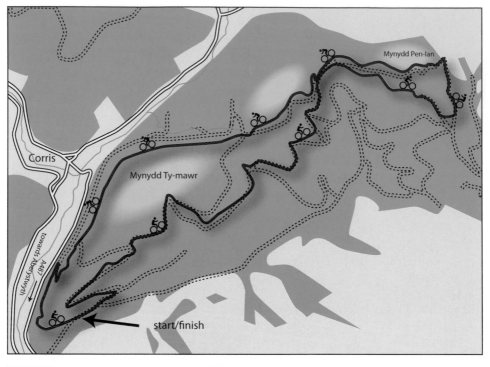

Mynydd Pen-lan

Corris

Mynydd Ty-mawr

towards Aberystwyth

A487

start/finish

ride well, it's just somewhat lacking in features.

The trail opens out and you're on what must be an old forest road. The surface is loose and you climb up through the trees and join another forest road, linking to another single-track section before popping over the ridgeline and onto what seems to be the dark side of the hill. We rode this trail in the spring and you could tell that there was still not much light getting to this side of the hill as the trail was damp and slow-running in places. You will end up back on a forest road traversing around the north side of the hill before arriving at the diagonal crossroads where you climbed up on your outbound loop. Here you take

The loose surface and steep gradient will test the legs and skills

The last descent has some spectacular views. It is worth stopping to savour the delights of the surrounding countryside

the switchback right and climb up a rough steep trail.

At the top of the climb the trail swings left to enter quite a dense plantation that traverses the hillside. Before starting to descend you will pass across a forest road and into another section of single track.

You are about to enter what has been dubbed as the longest single-track descent in Wales, and personally I feel it delivers on its promise. Throughout this section you will encounter switchback turns, blind crests, rocky drops, natural bedrock sections to traverse across (not quite all descending!) and all the other ingredients a fantastic piece of single track should have. At some point in this descent it is worth coming to a stop and appreciating the view down the valley and to the village of Corris below. Throughout the lower section of trail there are some tight switchbacks and one particular blind right-hand corner over an outcrop of rock that requires nerves of steel to take at speed. When you exit this fantastic trail you join a forest road taking a left turn. In the blink of an eye you're back at the car, hopefully desperate for more.

103

COED-Y-BRENIN

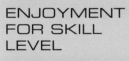

FACILITIES

Car park and charges: Yes; charges apply

Cafe: Yes

Toilets: Yes

Showers: Yes

Bike wash: Yes

Nearest bike shop: On site

Bike hire: Yes, on site

Accommodation: Hotels, B&Bs, self-catering log cabins and campsites in and around the area. The nearest town of Dolgellau has most amenities.

Other trails on site: 1x Green (Yr Afon), 1x Blue (MinorTaur – Loop 1), 3x Red (Temtiwr, Dragons Back, Cyflym Coch), 2x Black (Beast of Brenin, Tarw).

Ordnance Survey map: Explorer OL 18 combined with OL23 to cover a larger area to the east.

ENJOYMENT FOR SKILL LEVEL

Beginner: 6/10

Intermediate: 10/10

Advanced: 10/10

Getting there: The forest centre is located approximately 8km north of Dolgellau on the A470.

Grid ref: SH 72320 26917

Sat nav: LL40 2HY

More info: www.mbwales.com

MINORTAUR: BLUE LOOPS 1 & 2

On-site grade: Blue

Clive's grade: Blue/Green

Distance: 5.5km

Technicality: 3–4/10

Ascent: 95m

ENJOYMENT FOR SKILL LEVEL

Beginner: 10/10

Intermediate: 6/10

Advanced: 4/10

Coed-y-Brenin visitor centre

The new-built Blue trail takes in the lower slopes of the main Coed-y-Brenin forest and offers less-experienced riders a taste of what lies out in the larger landscape.

From the visitor centre drop in behind the centre and pick up the trail which starts with a large metal ring. The trail winds its way across the hill through the trees before taking a couple of uphill switchback turns. You will pass by an abandoned stone building before descending into a series of small jumps and bermed corners. The surface is smooth but loose gravel sits just off the ride line so keep it on line to avoid sliding out.

The trail joins on to a forest road and after a few metres turns left up a single-track climb. Here you will have a set of switchbacks to deal with before traversing around the front of the hill heading down towards the river. At

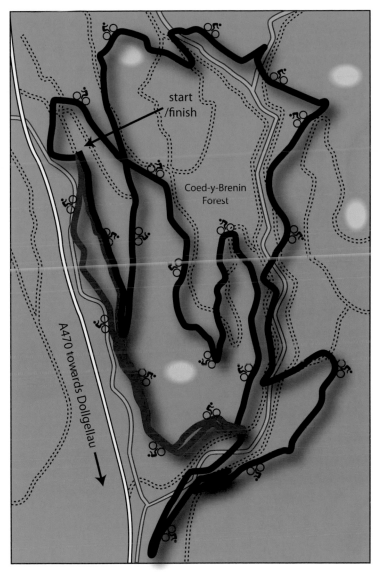

the end of this section there are some more flowing turns and you will be linked on to a public road which you follow for a few metres before turning right.

At this point you may want to take a look at the gorge. The bridge over the gorge is the main link to the majority of the other trails in the forest. The Blue route continues to run back on itself with the river down to your left before crossing the public road again to join into a forest road. The forest road runs along the bottom of the hill and you have nice views of the river down to your left. When you are at the top of the climb there is a small piece of trail to link you back to the visitor centre.

The latest feature at Coed-y-Brenin: an easy-going, fun and flowing Blue-grade trail

▶ MBR

On-site grade: Black

Clive's grade: Black/Red

Distance: 18km

Technicality: 9/10

Ascent: 525m

ENJOYMENT FOR SKILL LEVEL

Beginner: 3/10

Intermediate: 7/10

Advanced: 10/10

A fine trailhead monument, these monster forks mark the start of the more technical trails

From the visitor centre take the outbound trail starting through the giant front forks. This opening section is very rough, as the ground is made up of large stones and bedrock, and is a good indicator as to whether you will enjoy or have to endure the rest of the ride.

At the end of this section you will join a tarmac road where you need to take a switchback left and climb uphill. The gradient is quite steep and there's more climbing beyond the tarmac. The road eventually turns into a gravel track and you continue to climb heading up into the treeline where you will join another forest road on a switchback. Continue straight ahead.

When you crest the hill you will notice that your return trail is on your left-hand side. Continue straight ahead along the forest road for another few hundred metres before turning right and climbing on a narrow single-track trail. The surface is rough and loose: this is a fun technical section where grip is scarce. At the top you will join a forest road where you will take a right turn. This is the final piece of climbing for the moment. As you crest the hill a single-track trail appears on your right-hand side and it's time to get some reward for all the climbing.

The first part and final parts of the descent are very rough in places and you have a few rocky drops to deal with. At the end of the first section take a left turn and roll down the forest road for a few metres

This rocky section will require your full concentration

Exiting the river at the top of this ramp, take a left turn and almost immediately turn right up another steep section of rough technical trail. You'll crest the hill with open ground to your left and the trail levels out. Here you get a brief chance to recover before crossing a small stream and turning right into a section of single track.

The following section of trail flows down the hillside and there are a few split-line options: be aware of some tight turns and one particularly large bomb hole which, at the time of riding, was holding a deep puddle. The latter stages of this single track will lead you down to the forest road running parallel to the main river.

The deep gorge is a key feature of the forest

before taking a switchback right into another section of single track.

This section of trail has a different feel from the other part. It is newly built, smooth surfaced and consists of jumps and bermed turns but the modern heavily manufactured style to the trail just does not sit right with the rest of the forest. At the end you will join a forest road, take a right turn and after a few metres turn left into another piece of single track. Unfortunately this section is short-lived and you pop back out onto a forest road where you continue to descend to a bridge.

Cross the bridge and climb up slightly before turning right into a single track. This section has recently been clear-felled and as a consequence the trail has now become heavily eroded and is very rough and narrow. You will also find a few sizeable drops through this section and some tight switchback turns before crossing another bridge and climbing up out on a steep double track.

More rock drops and boulders in the final descent

Once on the lower forest road with the river to your right catch your breath because in no time at all you'll be taking a left turn and climbing up on a steep forest road. You will come up out of the trees into the open with fields up to your left. Just a few more metres of climbing to go before you turn right into a section of single track. This section will traverse the hillside descending slightly. Those of you that have ridden here before may recognise some of this from the original Karrimore loop. Once again you join to the lower forest road but this time you will have done a switchback so the river will be to your left-hand side.

Follow the forest road back up to the main bridge that links all trails in the forest, cross the bridge, take a right turn and ride along the public road with the river to your right for a few hundred metres. At the time of riding it looked like there were new trail developments up to our left. I can envisage that in no time at all there will be single-track trails linking to the next climb, taking you off the public road.

The final climb is on a forest road. Here the gradient is relatively steep in parts. The section following the climb is also quite undulating and has a few small ramps that will deal tired legs a bit of a blow. There are some fantastic views on offer as you climb and traverse the hillside. When you crest the hill continue to follow the forest road until you get to your final section of single track.

The last section of trail is very rough and rocky, you will need to use all your skills in order to navigate your way to the bottom safely. The trail takes a tight twist and crosses over the entrance to the car park. If you are tired at this stage you can opt out, alternatively there are still a few more metres of descending left and continuing straight over, linking up the final stages down to the river below the visitor centre. To complete the trail climb up back past the visitor centre looping round past the bike wash, bike shop and cafe back into the main car park.

CWMCARN

►FACILITIES

Car park and charges: Yes; free

Cafe: Yes

Toilets: Yes

Showers: No

Bike wash: Yes

Nearest bike shop: PS Cycles, Bridge Street, Abercarn, Gwent, NP11 4SE (01495 272001)

Bike hire: No

Accommodation: Campsite in the forest and nearby towns have B&B and hotel accommodation.

Other trails on site: Bridleways and permissive forest roads.

Ordnance Survey map: Explorer 152.

ENJOYMENT FOR SKILL LEVEL

Beginner: 4/10

Intermediate: 8/10

Advanced: 8/10

Getting there: Take junction 28 from the M4 and head north on the A467. Follow the signs for Cwmcarn Forest Drive. Carry straight on until the fifth roundabout and turn right, then turn right again. Cwmcarn Forest Drive is the second entrance on your left.

Grid ref: ST 22968 93558

Sat nav: NP11 7FA

More info: www.mtbwales.com www.cwmdown.co.uk

►TWRCH TRAIL

On-site grade: Red

Clive's grade: Red

Distance: 13.5km

Technicality: 6/10

Ascent: 426m

ENJOYMENT FOR SKILL LEVEL

Beginner: 5/10

Intermediate: 8/10

Advanced: 7/10

The cafe and visitor centre

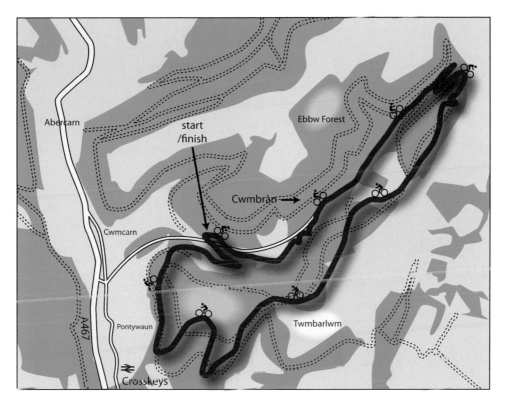

The trail starts at the top right-hand side of the car park. Climb up, traversing the hill in open ground. Take your time here as it's a considerable climb broken down into four sections. You will pass under the downhill track and continue climbing up to a wooden pinch fence. Go straight through and into the next section where the trail traverses the hill and crosses a footpath before descending into a tight left-hand switchback. Be careful on the exit of this switchback as the surface is very loose and you need to take a tight right turn. There is a fence on the outside of the corner and the trail goes through another pinch gate.

Crossing over and through another pinch fence traverse the hill and start to descend down to the forest drive. There are some boulders to control your speed as you come onto the forest drive here, turn right and aim to the left of the ticket booth and through a pinch fence. The trail now climbs up a gully on the right-hand side with the stream down to your left, throughout this section there are some rough climbs and steep gradients, so take your time and save your legs for the latter part of the climb.

The trail traverses the side of the gully and crosses over at a small bridge, the gradient from this point on eases slightly but there are still some tight steep rough sections ahead. Switching back over the stream you now climb up through steep switchbacks and out onto the forest drive. Be aware of cars approaching from the right. Continue straight ahead and up another single-track section, switching back up the hill before levelling out and crossing the forest drive once more. Here there will be a small car park and picnic area on your left as you head straight over, passing around a metal gate and up a forest road.

Within a few metres the trail turns right and climbs up a single track. This section is quite rough and you traverse back across the hillside with the forest road and forest drive down to your right. There is a steep rise at the end of this section which brings you out onto an old forest road where you need to switchback left and continue to climb. The hill levels out and you will see a fence on your left heading into a single track.

This is also the start of the freeride/jump loop. There are various lines through this section which you can take, some lines have jumps including double jumps and tabletops. After approximately 60 metres

the Red trail turns off to your right and the Black jump line is straight on. The Red trail is a fast-flowing section and it's well worth another loop back up through the car park and forest road climb to start this section again. If you choose to take the Black option line then you will be in for a treat: the jumps are relatively small and are easily achievable. The trails converge next to a fence on your right and a car park on the forest drive. (There is a small pinch gate where you can cut out and head back up through the car park passing a metal gate and continuing on a forest track, at the top of the climb you will see the entrance to the section on your right.)

To continue on the cross-country loop, descend down on a narrow single track with a fence to your right and the forest drive down below you. This is a fast section

The Welsh landscape viewed from the top of the first climb

The speed is quite high on this narrow descent

The small red directional arrows can be hard to see at speed

but beware as there is a left-hand turn at the end that tightens up with no support on the exit! From here the trail climbs up through the trees. The gradient is relatively easy but this trail does have a sting in the tail, so again try and conserve energy throughout this section. As you traverse the hill the trail starts to gather momentum. This section has eroded into a gully and the surface is loose.

In the final stages of this descent you'll be out in the open and riding in the gully. Take care and be aware at the bottom of this section as there is a hard 90° left-hand corner which leads into a steep climb. The climb has been concreted and will need a low gear. At the top here the forest drive will be on your right-hand side and a footpath on your left, the trail goes

through another pinch gate and traverses the hill. You should take a moment to get your breath and savour the lovely view in front of you as you pass through the pinch gate. After a short distance of climbing on mellow gradients you start to descend. This is not the final descent as there is still one small climb to deal with.

The final descent can get very fast and is quite rough in places. Be aware after several hundred metres of descending you will come to a pinch gate, after the gate you descend and join into a forest road, follow the forest road for a few metres before turning left through a gap in a fence. The trail drops down over some whoops and swings right into a large left-hand berm. The final blast consists of several blind crests, take care here as the bike will go light

The long traverse round the hill to the final blast down to the car park

▶DOWNHILL TRAILS

Clive's grade: Orange/Black

Distance: N/A

Technicality: Downhills, 7–8/10

ENJOYMENT FOR SKILL LEVEL

Beginner: 5/10

Intermediate: 8/10

Advanced: 7/10

and want to slide out from underneath you! Also be aware that it is easy to run wide on the exit of the turns.

At the bottom of this section the trail levels out into a very tight right-hand switchback. A few more metres of trail and you enter a tight left-hand switchback with a pinch gate – those of you with wide handlebars will struggle to get through this gate. There is one more switchback to go round and a tight turn runs between some boulders into the lower end of the car park.

The downhill trails are frequently used for competitions. They comprise of bermed turns, blind crests, drop offs, jumps and sections that you have to commit to. There is an uplift service that runs on a regular basis. You can find detailed information on this in the car park and on the website. You will also find plenty of videos on YouTube where you can get a rider's-eye view of the trails.

Uplifts are available for the downhill tracks

NANT YR ARIAN

▶ FACILITIES

Car park and charges: Yes; charges apply

Cafe: Yes

Toilets: Yes

Showers: No

Bike wash: Yes

Nearest bike shop: Summit Cycles, 65 North Parade Aberystwyth, Ceredigion, SY23 2JN (01970 626061)

Bike hire: No

Accommodation: Lots of B&Bs in the area. Aberystwyth is a large town and offers, among other things, shops, fuel, pubs and restaurants.

Other trails on site: Red and Black.

Ordnance Survey map: Explorer 213.

ENJOYMENT FOR SKILL LEVEL

Beginner: 6/10

Intermediate: 10/10

Advanced: 7/10

Getting there: The trails are located at the forest centre 16km east of Aberystwyth on the A44.

Grid ref: SN 71790 81411

Sat nav: SY23 3AD

More info: www.forestry.gov.uk/bwlchnantyrarian

▶ SUMMIT TRAIL

On-site grade: Red

Clive's grade: Red

Distance: 14km

Technicality: 6/10

Ascent: 440m

ENJOYMENT FOR SKILL LEVEL

Beginner: 6/10

Intermediate: 10/10

Advanced: 7/10

Trailhead information is located in the upper car park

The colour of the trail signs do not represent the grade

The trail opens with a mellow forest road climb, at the top of the forest road turn left into a single-track section named The Italian Job. This is an absolutely fantastic piece of trail, snaking down the hillside through a series of open corners and switchbacks.

At the bottom of The Italian Job you will join a forest road where you take a right turn and climb up. This is the same forest road that you will climb up on your return leg.

As you crest the hill the forest road drops down and you will join a public road. You get a quick chance to relax the legs and catch a breath before turning left into a nice technical rocky section of single track. The section is short but sweet. Once you rejoin the public road, continue on for approximately 200m and turn left through a gate.

You now climb up on a 4x4 track on an open hilltop. Once you have crested the hill the trail starts to descend. This section is quite rough and loose and there are a few water gullies to navigate through. You will also go through a series of gates and after the final gate you join a forest road where you take a left turn and continue descending.

Keep an eye out for a single-track trail on your right. This is another superb piece of trail, and you really get the feel-good factor as you flow across the hillside. The section that follows is named The Mark of Zorro, and once again you are on another amazing piece of single track.

After you have navigated your way down one of the longest single-track descents in the British Isles, you blend into a forest road and start the long climb back up to the top

The view down the valley on The Italian Job

of the hill. Partway up the forest road climb you will be directed left into a section of single track: this twists and traverses the hillside and you will continue to climb before rejoining the forest road. Once back on the forest road, continue to climb and you will soon be back on the section you rode on the outbound trail. At the false summit the outbound trail goes straight on, take a right turn here and continue to climb on the forest road. You will reach a junction on your left into a single-track trail.

You're into the final few kilometres of the trail now and you do get a small reward for all the climbing with another flowing section of trail. Beyond the single track you will be on another forest road with the final rise to deal with. The gradient here is quite steep but hopefully you have not gone too hard on the long forest road climb and you have enough energy left to power your way over the top.

The final sections of single track are great fun: fast-flowing corners twist along the hillside and bring you back to the visitor centre and car park.

Some sections are smooth and fast

117

PENMACHNO

Penmachno with its stunning backdrop

▶FACILITIES

Car park and charges: Yes; free

Cafe: No

Toilets: No

Showers: No

Bike wash: No

Nearest bike shop: Tan Lan/Holyhead Rd, Betws-y-Coed, LL24 0AB (01690 710766)

Bike hire: From above shop, nothing available on site

Accommodation: B&Bs, hotels, camping and all amenities in nearby Llanrwst and Betws-y-Coed.

Other trails on site: Natural trails/permissive paths and forest tracks.

Ordnance Survey map: Explorer OL17.

ENJOYMENT FOR SKILL LEVEL

Beginner: 3/10

Intermediate: 10/10

Advanced: 8–9/10

Getting there: From the A5 just south of Betws-y-Coed take a left-turn sign posted to Penmachno. Go through the village and a few hundred metres beyond you will see a forest road entrance to your right. Drive up the forest and park up by the trailhead.

Grid ref: SH 78658 49810

Sat nav: Penmachno

More info: www.mbwales.com

▶ LOOP 1

On-site grade: Red

Clive's grade: Red

Distance: 18.5km

Technicality: 7/10

Ascent: 580m

ENJOYMENT FOR SKILL LEVEL

Beginner: 3/10

Intermediate: 10/10

Advanced: 8–9/10

Penmachno offers you the choice of two Red-graded trails, the second trail is an extension to the first loop and shares the outbound single track and forest roads. Tt comprises of more single track and forest roads and joins up and returns with Loop 1.

From the car park climb up the steep forest road. This initial climb seems to be a running theme with Welsh trails and can be quite a brutal start to anyone's day. The forest road takes a right-hand switch and continues to climb. Here you're presented with some fantastic views as you climb up the hillside.

Take a left turn and crest the hill with open fields to your right. The first section of single-track climb will be up to your left. This section traverses the hill and continues to climb before dropping down to join a forest road. Climb up the forest road for a few metres and take a single-track trail on your right.

The single track hugs the hillside and in dense pine plantation you traverse along before rejoining another forest road. The waymarkings at this point are very good and they will guide you up the forest road for a few metres. Right turn onto another forest road then left turn into a single

Small red arrows show you the way

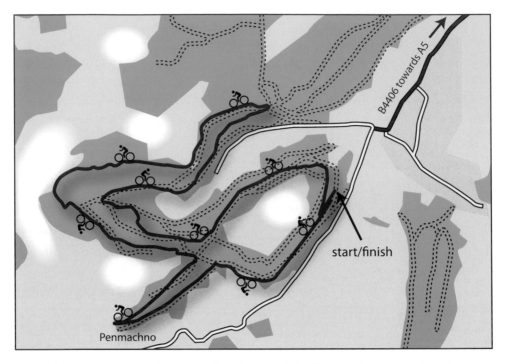

track. This section is running around and dropping down the hillside. The trail is narrow and some of the corners tighten up on themselves so be on your guard! The section is mainly downhill but there are a good few parts that require some physical effort. Be careful not to overdo it here as you will join a rough old disused forest road at the end of this single track and climb up quite a steep gradient to a crossroads.

When you arrive at these crossroads you are in the open and have spectacular views of the hill in front of you. Traverse around the hillside in front of you on the return stages of the trail. At the crossroads take a right turn and roll along the forest road. After a few hundred metres a single track on your right drops downhill.

The trail gets very fast in places and it is quite narrow with blind crests – the typical Welsh whoops and jumps make you work

hard. You'll pass close to the forest road a couple of times throughout this section. When you reach the forest road for the third time the section is over and it's back to climbing.

The forest road climb has a mellow gradient but it is quite a long section. You come out into the open at the top of the forest road and the trail turns off to the right and continues to climb. You now traverse the hillside that you were looking up at from a crossroads junction earlier on. The trail here is heavily eroded from both riders and the weather: the surface is rough and loose and you have to be strong to get the most out of this section.

You will eventually drop down. There are some large bedrock sections to deal with followed by a short but tough little climb. Back into single track and the pace will really start to pick up. An eroded gully

Sweeping single track switches up the steep hillside

leads down the hillside into a series of tight switchbacks before joining another forest road. The forest road runs round the hillside and you come out into the open with a single-track trail signposted to your left.

Here you have superb views back up the valley and in the distance you will see the slate mine cut into the hillside. Once again you have a fast section of descent with blind crests and large whoops. At the bottom of this section you blend into a forest road that climbs back up the hillside, taking a right turn at a T-junction and traversing the hill for a few hundred metres before you turn right into the final single-track descent.

The final descent is awesome, tight switchbacks, rock drops, exposure, jumps: it's got the lot! At the end a short steep ramp pops you back out into the car park and leaves you asking the question: should we do that again?

The long traverse makes its way down the hill, this section can be hard graft on a windy day

▶ALSO WORTH RIDING

COED LLANDEGLA

Cross-country trails, 5km Green, 12km Blue, 18km Red with 2km Black options. Jump spot, skills area and pump track

Camping, hotels and B&Bs in the area

Bike shop, bike hire cafe and toilets on site

Location: Take the A525 from Wrexham to Ruthin and exit when signposted into a narrow lane, the main car park is a few kilometres up the lane.

Grid ref: SJ227520

Sat nav: LL11 3AA

Info: www.coedllandegle.com

COED TRALLWM

Cross country trails, 4km Blue, 5km Red and 6km Black

Camping, hotels and B&Bs in the area

Bike shop, bike hire cafe and toilets on site

Location: Take the A40 from Llandovery heading west, turn right onto the A483 towards Builth Wells, in Beulah turn left onto a minor road heading towards Abergwesyn. The trail-head is approximately 7km up the lane.

Grid ref: SN 882543

Sat nav: LD5 4TS

Info: www.coedtrallwm.co.uk

SCOTLAND

AE FOREST

Car park and charges: Yes; charges apply

Cafe: Yes

Toilets: Yes

Showers: Yes

Bike wash: Yes

Nearest bike shop: On site

Bike hire: Yes

Accommodation: B&Bs, hotels, self-catering accommodation and camping around the area, all amenities in nearby Dumfries.

Other trails on site: Green, Blue, Orange DH, permissive paths and forest roads.

Ordnance Survey map: Explorer 321.

ENJOYMENT FOR SKILL LEVEL

Beginner: 4/10

Intermediate: 6/10

Advanced: 8/10

Getting there: Ae Forest is located next to Ae village just off the A701 trunk road. From Dumfries, head north towards Moffat (and the M74) on the A701; you will see the brown signs pointing you left to Ae Forest/village. Just under 4km down the country lane you enter the village and will see signs on your right for the forest. The main car park is located just over the bridge on your left-hand side. There is also an overflow car park and trailhead, which is found by continuing straight on to the T-junction, taking a left turn and following the forest road over the cattle grid and through the field. You will go over a second cattle grid before turning left into the overflow car park.

Grid ref: NX 98453 89503

Sat nav: DG1 1QB

More info: www.7stanesmountainbiking.com

▶ THE ORIGINAL AVALANCHE ENDURO LOOP

▶ AE LINE (XC RED) AND SHREDDER (ORANGE FREERIDE LINE)

On-site grade: Red

Clive's grade: Red with Black sections

Distance: 26.6km

Technicality: 7.5/10

Ascent: 743m

ENJOYMENT FOR SKILL LEVEL

Beginner: 2/10

Intermediate: 5/10

Advanced: 8/10

Ae Forest is steeped in Scottish mountain bike history as the venue has been host to countless Scottish National and British National race events. The venue was also host to the inaugural round of the Avalanche Enduro series and was the second venue in the British Isles to host a stage-based gravity event.

Starting from the first car park near the forestry office, follow the signs along the gravel track for a few metres before joining a forest road. Keeping the open field to your left, head down to a T-junction and take a left turn following the forest track through the field. On your right-hand side you will see the infamous road gap on the downhill course and the large bank where riders descend into Fred's Field.

At the end of the field, pass over a second cattle grid and turn left into the overflow car park. Once in the car park take the second right turn and continue straight

Ae Forest

along past another trailhead sign into a smooth double-track section that runs parallel with the river. Take a left turn, cross the river and ride up to a forest road. On the opposite side of the forest road you enter a single-track climb.

This initial climb is quite steep and can easily deprive you of energy, which

Art in the outdoors; this bench depicts the history of Ae Forest

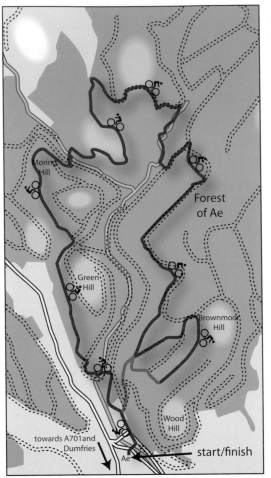

you will certainly need further round the lap. Clinging to the hillside you twist and traverse up through a series of switchbacks. The trail levels out, giving you a quick chance to catch a breath before completing the final few switchbacks up into the trees and out onto a forest road. The final section does have some desire lines and you could be tempted to cut across left onto the forest road early – but avoid adding to the scar on the landscape by sticking to the main trail joining the forest road just a few metres further up.

Once on the forest road descend slightly and fork off right into another single track. Traverse the hillside and link to another section of single track. This drops down slightly as it traverses around the hill. You will come out into

The opening climb was used as a descent in the Avalanche Enduro, its quite a brutal start to a ride with steep gradients and tight switchbacks

the open and drop down through a large dip that leads you into a series of uphill switchbacks. This is one area on the trail where it's easy to get caught out and end up in a large gear as you climb up into the tight and steep switchback turns. After the first of the switchbacks the trail dips down once again before climbing up through another set of steep switchbacks. After the second set the trail really opens up and you get a good few metres of descent before another short rise leads you into the final section of the single track and down to a forest road.

Climbing up the forest road to the 5-ways junction, take a left turn and continue to climb on the forest road before you branch off left into a section of single track named Granny Green Love. The initial section of trail has been resurfaced and is relatively uneventful. You can carry much more speed through the turns since the resurfacing and this has made the corners a little more of a challenge.

The surface changes and becomes rough, and a small tabletop leads you out into the open before you climb up over some sizeable stone sets. As you crest this small rise a couple of rock drops put you into the main downhill of Granny Green Love. At the time of riding the descent was quite rough and the potential for pinch-punctures quite high: during the Avalanche Enduro event many people suffered from punctured tyres and dented wheels throughout this section.

As well as rough ground you will also have some large tabletop jumps, a step-up–step-down jump and some very rough berms to deal with. A rock drop 'fly off' jump leads you at high speed across a forest road

and into the final section. Once again the surface is rough. A series of small rock drops leads you into a run of large steep berms: the first berm has a rough rock drop on its entrance and the trail surface here is heavily eroded. The final section of trail has been rebuilt but the smoother surface is still very loose. Take care as you descend through the final corners and onto the narrow bridge!

Beyond the bridge you enter a climber named The Face. Here the trail surface is very rough and rocky. A steep climb switches up the hillside through a series of tight switchbacks. Once you have climbed up through the three switchbacks the trail then traverses the hill continuing to climb slightly. At the end of the traverse you switch left and the gradient increases once more as you climb up through the trees. Just before you exit the trees a tight left-hand corner leads you into a rock-paved section. This section is exceptionally tricky in the wet and is no walk in the park in the dry!

Rough sections of trail on Granny Green Love really push the grade

After the climb, a freshly surfaced section of trail winds its way across the hilltop and out into open ground. The trail descends slightly before climbing across an old quarry, taking a left turn up a double track. You will traverse across an open hillside and onto Bran Burn Bash. The surface here used to be very rough and it was hard to keep your speed on some of the uphill sections. The trail has since been resurfaced and the going is much faster. There is some good movement to the trail and some nice fast corners to keep you entertained, but take care as a few of these turns do tighten up!

Bran Burn Bash joins into a forest road and you descend for a few more metres before switching right and climbing up on the opposite side of the valley. Depending on your fitness levels this climb can be quite a challenge as the moderate-to-steep gradient is sustained for a considerable distance. When you get to the top of the forest road you'll come to a T-junction, straight ahead is a Black option line which involves a couple of hundred metres of

Many sections have been resurfaced and now roll fast

raised wooden boardwalks. There are no nasty corners or hidden surprises in this section, it is graded Black as a precaution. For those of you who are not keen on raised wooden boardwalks take the right turn and follow the forest road for a couple of hundred metres before branching off to the left and rejoining the trail at the end of the boardwalk.

Beyond the boardwalk the trail climbs up slightly through a series of switchbacks before entering the start of the descent named The Edge. The opening section of trail is smooth and very fast. A series of fast sweeping corners lead you down to a step-up jump with a sizeable downslope landing beyond it – you may want to inspect it before you ride it! There is the option of taking a trail to the left and running around the top of the bomb hole, thus avoiding the step-up jump.

The Edge snakes its way through the trees and there are some quite tight gaps for those of you with wider handlebars. You then cross over a forest road and into open ground where another series of fast corners leads you down to a large long right-hand berm into The Edge proper. Run along the top of a very large bank with the river below you and to your left. On this tight single-track section, twist your way around old tree stumps before the gradient steepens and two sets of switchbacks drop you down and over a small wooden bridge into a short sharp climb. Raced in its entirety this section really does get the legs and lungs burning.

After the steep gradient the trail descends again, and runs parallel to the river before climbing up and levelling out. It then descends through a series of blind crests

The Edge

and tightening corners. The final section drops down a steep bank and a couple of tight rough switchbacks lead you into the final straight on to a boardwalk and over a bridge. A short climb up out the other side links you on to a forest road – this is one of the few points where you can cut back to the car park (by taking a right-hand turn).

Take a left turn on the forest road and continue to climb up to a junction on your right-hand side. The forest road continues to climb for a short distance before a single track heads off to your right; you'll continue to climb for another couple of hundred metres before dipping down to twist around the hillside. This section cuts the corner of the forest road and a short climb up through a couple of switchbacks pops you out onto the forest road where you take the right turn.

Follow the forest road, dipping down and climbing up slightly before arriving at the headstone and the start to Omega Man.

There are some spectacular views here and it's a popular spot where riders stop to catch their breath before the final few descents.

The Omega Man is a rough narrow single-track trail that descends through some cheeky corners before climbing up the hillside. After this first short climb the trail starts to descend again and will lead you down to a small wooden bridge and a short steep climb up through a series of switchbacks.

The trail levels out beyond the switchbacks, linking you to the next section of the descent. Blind crests and small jumps ease you in before the speed picks up and you really get going. Fast corners, whoops and a series of super-smooth flowing berms lead down through a break in the trees. Here the surface changes and a rough right-hand switchback drops you through a large dip with a tough little climb on the exit.

Climb up on a double track beyond the dip for a few hundred metres and you will

The headstone at the start of Omega Man, views out to the Solway Coast and Criffel

arrive at a junction on the trail. The Red XC route is signposted to the right. This is the final section of the trail which pops you out back at the overflow car park (and the push up for The Shredder). I rode the original Avalanche Enduro loop, which involves going straight past the junction and taking a switchback left onto the forest road, picking up the signs for The Shredder.

▶ TRAIL 2: THE SHREDDER

You need to follow the forest road climbing up for just over 2.5km. Pass a couple of forest roads on your right and continue to a T-junction where you'll be signed right climbing up a short steeper section of forest road before you turn right again around a metal gate. The final section of climb leads to a fast short descent past a turning

circle and up into a narrower double track. Beyond the rough double track there is a gravel area and some signage. The Shredder trail was the final stage of the Avalanche Enduro and the start is to your right – this is well signed and easy to find.

Shredder is an easier option to the main downhill track. Here you encounter jumps, drops, a road gap, fast berms and rough surfaces. After the initial couple of rock drops a 90° left leads you into a switchback right. When you exit this switchback there is the option of dropping down to your left (this section is steep and rough) or you can continue straight on to a boardwalk and into a very tight left-hand switchback. This boardwalk section can become very slippery in the wet and the tight section in the trees has some large exposed roots and a few narrow rock drops to contend with.

As you exit the trees and rejoin the main line you come to the first in a series of drop-offs. Full commitment is needed as some of these can't be rolled down! Beyond the first drop the ride line tightens and sweeps to the right before a series of tight corners leads you into The Road Gap, this is not for the fainthearted! The gap is not particularly large in either its height or distance but the landing area is small. The corners on the run-up also hinder your ability to carry a decent speed into the feature: it is critical to get a good exit on the corners and maintain enough momentum to guarantee landing in the downslope rather than on the forest road. There is an alternative option line to the right of the drop and if you're not sure then make sure you have a look before you leap!

Beyond The Road Gap a small set of doubles leads you into some tight turns and small drops. The trail continues in a similar vein and there are a couple of cheeky tabletops between tight bermed corners. The style of the trail changes as you start to exit the trees: a sneaky off-camber corner could easily catch you out if you let your guard down. After the off-camber section a switchback right puts you into a couple of nice jumps before joining into a forest road. Climb up slightly on the forest road and follow the trail down to your left before taking a very tight left-hand switchback into the final section of Shredder/Omega Man. When you exit the tight left-hand switchback make sure you are on the trail on the left-hand side as the wider trail on the right is the push-up path.

This final descent is a fantastic blast and a superb way to finish a great ride. The surface is heavily eroded and rough, there are multiple blind crests, sizeable rock and tabletop jumps and it's guaranteed to put a

The road gap on Shredder has an awkward approach, there is an option line to the right that can be rolled down

smile on your face. Just after you enter the treeline the trail splits.

The Black option line to your left passes over to large sets of doubles, dropping down through a large bomb hole into a sizeable tabletop.

The Red option to the right passes over a smaller tabletop, which is followed by a square-edged drop-off that can't be rolled! Beyond the drop-off you pass through a large bomb hole and a small tabletop on the exit leads you into a left-hand corner where the Black option line blends in.

A series of blind crests and tabletops lead out the final section. Take care on the last few whoops as the speed is very high through this section.

At the bottom of the downhill there is another split-line option: the Black option to your left takes in skinny log rides and you will have to commit to a drop-off at the end of the logs into a tight right-hand turn!

The Red option joins into a boardwalk and onto the forest road (look out for vehicles on this forest road). To get back to the main car park simply follow the forest road, retracing your steps across open ground and taking a junction right at the end of the field. Head back up towards the forestry buildings and turn left back into the car park.

▶ DOWNHILL TRAILS

Clive's grade: Orange/Black

Distance: N/A

Technicality: 9/10

DOWNHILLS: ENJOYMENT FOR SKILL LEVEL

Beginner: 2/10

Intermediate: 6/10

Advanced: 10/10

There are a few variations to the main downhill track. From the summit cairn, the original line heads straight on down a steep bank before taking a left turn and traversing the hillside (to the left of the summit cairn there is a slightly newer line that was cut for a British national race, it simply rejoins the main line after a few hundred metres).

The first wooded section has multiple options. These trails will link up beyond the trees and lead you into the stream gap and a step-up jump, after which you have a split-line option at the next jump. Take the hip jump to the right and the trail switches left then right into a series of small drops before the road crossing. The line to the left will bring you down to the same road-crossing section. After a drop onto the forest road crossing, there are a few options down the main rock garden to the right or you can continue along the forest road for a few metres and drop in over a small gap jump into a double jump. Once again the trails merge into one line and after a few more metres you can turn off right and enter the lower wood.

Here you will find multiple split-line options that link into the final bank. The main line continues straight on over a set of doubles and into the infamous Coffin Jump. This is a gap jump with an option line to avoid the jump on the right. After the Coffin Jump the trail switches right and drops down into a set of tight switchbacks. Just before the switchbacks you can continue straight on into one of the many lines traversing the hill, and drop down the final bank to the infamous Road Gap. If you take the switchbacks and stick to the main line, traverse down the hillside where you have the option of splitting off left through a series of off-camber turns and missing the Road Gap Jump. After the gap jump a sizeable left-hand berm links to a large switch-right berm and into a double jump and left-hand switchback. You now simply traverse the hill and drop back down to the main forest road at the end of the field.

BALBLAIR – KYLE OF SUTHERLAND

▶ FACILITIES

Car park and charges: Yes; charges apply

Cafe: No

Toilets: No

Showers: No

Bike wash: No

Nearest bike shop: Various retailers in Inverness

Bike hire on site: None on site

Accommodation: B&Bs, hotels, self-catering accommodation and camping in and around the area. Bonar Bridge has most amenities.

Other trails on site: Blue.

Ordnance Survey map: Explorer 441.

ENJOYMENT FOR SKILL LEVEL

Beginner: 3/10

Intermediate: 5/10

Advanced: 8/10

Getting there: The trailhead is located on the north side of the A836 near the village of Bonar Bridge. Continue north-east on the main road beyond the village of Bonar Bridge for approximately 2km. You will see the forest entrance on your right-hand side.

Grid ref: NH 60375 93025

Sat nav: Bonar Bridge

More info: www.forestry.gov.uk

▶ TRAIL 1

On-site grade: Black

Clive's grade: Black

Distance: 8km

Technicality: 9/10

Ascent: 353m

ENJOYMENT FOR SKILL LEVEL

Beginner: 4/10

Intermediate: 6/10

Advanced: 8/10

Clear concise information, great signage at Balblair

Highland views nearing the top of the first climb

From the car park, continue up the tarmac road around the forest gate. After a short while turn right and climb up on a forest road. The opening section of trail is shared with the Blue. It is relatively wide and drops up and down as it cuts through the trees.

At the end of the section turn right on a forest road and climb for a short distance before turning left onto another forest road. When the forest road splits keep left and continue climbing. You will crest the hill and come out into the open. After a few metres, a single track on your right climbs up for a short distance.

You are now into the thick of the trail. The following kilometres consist of technical bedrock sections interspersed with narrow single track. There are numerous

Exposed bedrock makes for technical climbing

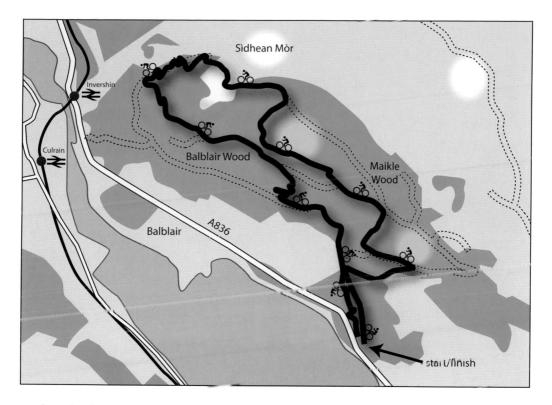

boardwalks to negotiate as well. On the rocks you will see painted arrows giving you the easiest option through the bedrock. This is a fantastic section in the trail and you can experiment with various ride lines as you roll over large open sections of bedrock.

Be careful, though, as some line choices may lead you astray and off away from the main trail. Partway through the section there is a short loop that you can add in – keep right for the main trail. At the end of this long section you will come on to a forest road/track turning right. Once again there is a shortcut option. The main Black trail continues round to the right climbing uphill.

This section is built from large pieces of rock and the gradient gets steeper as

the trail narrows down and you head up towards the next forest-road-link section. When you exit the rock slab climb, take a left turn on the forest road and traverse around the hillside.

Continue to follow the main forest road past the turning circle and climb up towards the radio mast. The trail turns right before the mast and the last few metres of climbing leads you up onto the hilltop. The next section is another mix of open bedrock and boardwalk. Partway down the descent you'll find a split-line option on the boardwalk. Keep to the right and continue to descend over bedrock and boardwalk.

A forest road link climbs back up the hill and ends in a section of single track that climbs up to your left. The climb is quite

Sections of boardwalk link bedrock

steep, the surface loose, and it makes a good technical climb. You start descending once more and open bedrock sections are linked with single track. Once again the surface can get quite loose so stay on your guard throughout this section.

At the bottom you will join a forest road and traverse the hillside with some spectacular views out to your right. At a clump of trees on your right you will enter one of the final sections of single track. This single track has some very tight corners and some quite severe rock drops. At the bottom of the single track, join a forest road linking you back to a section of shared trail. You are in the last stages of the descent back to the forest road where you started the loop. Simply retrace your steps back to the car park or head out and do it all again.

Bermed turns in the final descent

DALBEATTIE

▶ FACILITIES

Car park and charges: Yes; charges apply

Cafe: No

Toilets: No

Showers: No

Bike wash: Yes

Nearest bike shop: MPG Cycles, Millo Place, High Street, Dalbeattie. DG5 4DP (01556 610659)

Next Level Bikes, 21 St Andrew Street, Castle Douglas, DG7 1EL (01556 504698)

Bike hire: Yes, at MPG

Accommodation: B&Bs, hotels, self-catering accommodation and camping around the area. All amenities in nearby Dalbeattie, Castle Douglas and Dumfries.

Other trails on site: Green, Blue, Skills taster loops of all grades, permissive paths and forest tracks.

Ordnance Survey map: Explorer 313.

ENJOYMENT FOR SKILL LEVEL

Beginner: 6/10

Intermediate: 7/10

Advanced: 9/10

Getting there: From Dumfries take the A711 heading south-east for 23km to the small town of Dalbeattie. Pass through the town, past the petrol station and take the A710 Solway Coast road round the edge of town. You need to take the second forest entrance on the left in just under a kilometre.

Grid ref: NX 83625

Sat nav: Dalbeattie

More info: www.7stanesmountainbiking.com

▶ HARD ROCK TRAIL

On-site grade: Red

Clive's grade: Red with Black sections

Distance: 25.2km

Technicality: 8.5/10

Ascent: 718m

ENJOYMENT FOR SKILL LEVEL

Beginner: 2/10

Intermediate: 5/10

Advanced: 9/10

7stanes Key Information Point or KIP

139

From the trailhead signs, head outbound on all trails. Throughout this opening section of single track the trails are shared with the taster loops. There are some interesting option lines of various grades for you to experiment with. The Red-grade trail flows through the centre of some large granite outcrops, the Black-graded sections comprise of open bedrock with stone-pitched sections that link the large

Technical rock features on the opening sections are graded as Black-option lines

granite slabs. In the early days the slabs were very grippy, however, nowadays there is a lot less traction and caution should be taken on wet days as they can become exceptionally slippery!

After a few hundred metres of shared trail there is a short Red section to your left, then some fast sweeping corners lead you back onto the shared trail. Take your time in this section if it's your first time here and pay attention to the signs. There are trails running off left–right and you could easily end up making a short loop rather than heading out on the main outbound trail.

All trails head out on a smooth single track. After crossing the forest road you join a long section of boardwalk. This is the first of two sections of boardwalk – a short section of old forest road breaks up the two sections. At the end of the second section of boardwalk you join a forest road where you take a right turn climbing up to a T-junction, take a left turn and climb up

In a few hundred metres you start to rise up and you'll take a junction to your right, switching back before continuing to climb uphill. Once again the gradient levels out and a few hundred metres of level ground leads you into the final section of forest road climbing up to the Heart Stone. You will see the Heart Stone over to your right and a large granite slab on the opposite side poses an interesting challenge. The main trail runs past the bottom of this slab and through a nice section of single track out in the open.

At the end of the section a rock drop joins a single-track climb. The surface here is quite loose and the gradient quite steep. At the top of the climb, you pass through old woodland and there are a few interesting technical trail features to deal with before you enter the next descent.

The downhill is very fast and pretty rough. When the trail drops into an eroded water gully get ready as you will take a right turn dropping down a steep bank: the surface is loose and the opening section of bedrock is quite rough. At the bottom of this steep bank you join into a smoother single-track trail (shared with the Blue) and here you need to take a left turn.

The Blue trail takes a right turn and the Red continues straight ahead into a climb. This is quite steep, and on the exit to a left-hand switch-back the gradient steepens again as you ascend a short stone-pitched section. The trail levels out but only for a moment, then you're into another steep section climbing up onto a large piece of bedrock. Once again this is another physically demanding and technically challenging section of trail.

The Moyle Hill loop continues to twist its way around the hillside. There are plenty of small outcrops of rock and tight sections of trail. At the end of the Moyle Hill loop, traverse through gorse and out into the open to a forest road. Follow the forest road for a few hundred metres with spectacular views out to your right. You will get to a Black option line to your

right. This option line leads down to the infamous Slab.

If you decide to take this Black option line, you drop down a steep gradient over stone-pitching into a hard left-hand corner. A short straight links you to a tight right-hand turn up over an outcrop of rock and into the main slab drop. Care should be taken at the bottom of the slab as you need

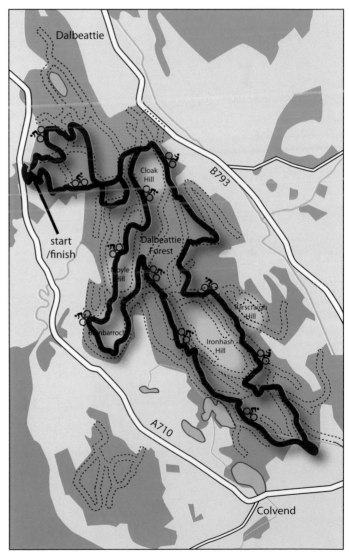

The Slab: take care at the bottom as the transition is quite harsh and the Red trail runs below

to make a hard right turn, and there may be riders approaching from your left.

There is also the option to avoid The Slab and take a turn into the right down a narrow section of single-track trail. If you do this expect exposed bedrock sections and rock drops. This trail also links back into the Red section that runs below the main Slab.

The main Red trail continues straight on along the forest road for another hundred metres before turning right and dropping down a rough single-track descent. You will pass the bottom of the Slab and a couple of rock-pinch gullys need to be negotiated before a stone-pitched section switchbacks down the hillside. The single track levels out and blends into a forest road.

The forest road link climbs up the hill. Take a junction to the right and almost immediately a junction to the left. The forest road has seen little use and a double-track trail narrows into single track. A short technical section drops down to a forest road over some stone-pitching, take a right and descend on the forest road.

You will fork off to the left over a stone-pitched bridge. This section is very fast and you can enter here with a lot of speed, so take care and slow down before turning off the forest road. The trail climbs up slightly and you have to work hard to maintain a decent speed on the rough surface. Partway along you will come to a sizeable rock drop. You can roll down this drop or you can launch off the top of it! If you have never ridden here before it's worth to take a look

Daria leads the local lads past some recently felled timber. You will see many of these while out riding as most forests are still operational. Obey all signage

before you leap as the surface is quite rough on the landing and the entrance blind. The trail continues in a similar vein and will link you back onto a forest road. Blend into the forest road and rest those legs.

You will come to a fork in the forest road where you need to take a left turn. You'll now be facing a steep gradient and staring up at a wide grey strip climbing up in front of you. When you crest this hill you will turn off to the right and into another section of single track. Once again the trail surface becomes quite rough in sections and there are large stone-pitched sections of trail for you to negotiate.

At the end of the section, a tight right-hand switchback brings you out onto an old forest road where you take a left turn at the T-junction. Continue to follow the old forest road to the turning circle at the end and take the single-track trail to your left, climbing up a short steep bank. This next section of trail links to The Terrible Twins and has a small climb into a short descent before another small climb. At the top of the hill you drop down and will have the Black option line down The Terrible Twins to your left.

The Terrible Twins are a pair of rock slab drops back-to-back. The gradient on each slab is reasonably steep and the exit to the second slab quite tricky. Rejoin the Red trail and take a hard left turn – it's imperative to control your speed on the entrance to both the rock slabs. This is a Black-graded section and can be avoided by continuing straight ahead on the single track and traversing the hill. At the time of riding there was an exposed section of bedrock just after a tight left-hand switchback that really pushed the grade into the next level.

The trail levels out and a single track joins into a forest road. Follow the forest road that climbs up around the hill. At the top you will come to a junction: take a left turn and continue to climb. The gradient here is very mellow and you get a good couple of kilometres to recover. Turn off the forest road and take a right turn into a single track. The trail comes out into the open and joins a disused forest road. This old forest road dips down and climbs up slightly before you come into the trees, arriving at Jacob's Ladder.

A tight right corner will lead you into a very steep stone-pitched section. Drop down over boulders and bedrock onto the stone-pitched run out. There is little room for error in this section and the overall look of the trail can be quite intimidating, especially in the wet! At the bottom of the stone-pitched descent a small kink to the right leads into a left-hand berm, the trail then blends back into a forest road.

You will follow the forest road for approximately 1km. The next section of single track will be on your right-hand side and is shared with the Blue trail. This is known as The Hyperlink. The Hyperlink joins into a forest road where you take a right turn. After a few metres take a junction off to the right and follow a forest track for a few hundred metres. This will peter out into a single-track trail, which is the start of Rock don't Roll.

Rock don't Roll only lasts for about 800m, but the gentle incline and rough surface make it a tough challenge. At the end of Rock don't Roll you will join a forest road, taking a tight switchback to the right. Continue on the forest road for approximately 1km before turning left up a rock

Rock don't Roll, a tough section for tired legs

slab into a single track. This short section links on to another forest road where you take a left turn. You will now be back at the junction where you headed outbound.

Continue straight ahead and retrace your steps along the forest road until you come to a junction on your left at the top of a small rise. Traverse around the hill on an old forest road. This will descend down and join into a more established forest road. Take care here as the speed is quite high and there could be other trail users on the forest road below!

The forest road descends round a tight right corner. After a short straight track you will take a fork to the left and be on famil-iar ground. This is where you headed out earlier in the lap. Within a few hundred metres the forest road bears round to the left and you will head straight on into a single-track section named The Instigator. This section of trail leads you up into some pine trees and a few technical rock features make for an interesting challenge when taken at speed. You will then come to a split-line option. For the main trail stick to the left, a Black option line goes on to a skinny log ride, the initial log links on to a section of bedrock where you have to take an awkward left turn down onto a narrower log.

A wooden bridge links into a series of switchbacks and up to the next split-line option at Shakey Jakey. The Red trail takes a left turn and snakes its way along the bottom of a large granite outcrop; the Black option line takes a right turn and climbs up a section of boardwalk onto a large slab of

There are many option lines across Shakey Jakey, a good place to stop and play

rock. When you come off of the boardwalk and onto the bedrock you have to take a tight right turn: this is off-camber and is a real challenge on a wet day. Shakey Jakey was named in memory of a dear friend of mine, Adam Jakeman.

On top of the rocky outcrop you will find skinny logs to negotiate. There are other options and alternative ways to drop down and rejoin the Red trail below. A short section of single track links to another split-line option, the Red trail on your right takes a drop-off and the Black option line to your left takes in a pinch gap between two large boulders and onto a skinny log ride. The trails blend together and a boardwalk section leads you on to a forest road where you take the right turn.

After a few metres on the forest road you take a left turn into another single-track section. This runs parallel to the forest road for approximately 100m before taking a left turn into the trees. Once again you will have another split-line option: the Black line to your left takes in a series of open bedrock sections and the Red trail to your right continues in a similar vein to the other single tracks. The lines converge as you come out into the open. Next up is another boardwalk. Here you will see to your left a Red-line option, this simply climbs up the bank over large root beds, traverses a few metres then drops back down to join into the trail you're currently on. It is a great short technical climb but only worth taking on if you think you have enough energy to make it.

The boardwalk links on to a single track. Heading back to the car park on a shared trail with the Blue. For this reason the trail

Shakey Jakey was named in memory of friend Adam Jakeman, a fitting headstone for a keen mountain biker

surfaces is much smoother than the rest of the trail. A short section of forest road brings you into the backside of the car park. You can either go round the gates in front of you to the far corner of the car park or take a single track on your left to return to the trailhead signage.

145

DRUMLANRIG

▶ FACILITIES

Car park and charges: Yes; charges apply (per person)

Cafe: Yes

Toilets: Yes

Showers: Yes

Bike wash: Yes

Nearest bike shop: On site

Bike hire: Yes

Accommodation: B&Bs, hotels, self-catering accommodation and camping around the area. Amenities in nearby Thornhill and Dumfries.

Other trails on site: Green, Blue, Black, permissive paths and estate roads.

Ordnance Survey map: Explorer 329.

ENJOYMENT FOR SKILL LEVEL

Beginner: 7/10

Intermediate: 9.5/10

Advanced: 7/10

Getting there: From Thornhill head north on the A76 for 4.5km. Pass through the village of Carronbridge and in just over 2km you will see the brown signs for the castle pointing left down a narrow lane. Follow the lane down the hill over the bridge and bear right, the car park is located to the right of the castle at the top of the drive.

Grid ref: NX 85087 99333

Sat nav: DG3 4AQ

More info: www.drumlanrig.com

▶ THE OLD SCHOOL

On-site grade: Red

Clive's grade: Red

Distance: 13.5km

Technicality: 8/10

Ascent: 330m

ENJOYMENT FOR SKILL LEVEL

Beginner: 3/10

Intermediate: 810

Advanced: 7/10

The trailhead is located at the upper end of the car park. Follow the red tarmac road over the cattle grid before turning right and climbing up an estate road (forest road). The climb is only short but the gradient can be a shock to cold muscles. As you crest the hill you will bear round to the left on a double track before turning left on another double track and almost immediately left again into single track.

This opening section of trail will give you a good idea of the type of technical trail features you're likely to find further round the loop. If you decide this is not for you it is advisable to cut out on one of the double tracks you cross while descending, head back to the car park and review your route selection: this trail is at the upper end of the grade. The single track traverses the hillside climbing slightly before descending through a series of switchbacks. The surface is rough in places and root beds, rocks, drops and tight turns are the order of the day.

After the second road crossing you will come to a split in the trail. The Red trail bears right and climbs up slightly before descending again to another estate road. Taking a right turn on this estate road, start to climb back up the hill. Once again the gradient is quite steep but the climb is not that long. Nearing the top of the hill you will come to a stone wall on your right and a 4-way junction. Bear round to the left and follow the trail as it continues to climb slightly (the trail is now single track).

A short climb switchbacks up the hill. At the top of the climb, run parallel to an estate road (you will return up this road having completed this next loop). The trail descends and you encounter some more tight switchbacks and large root beds throughout this section. There are also some parts that are quite rough and the gradient can get quite steep in places.

At the bottom of the descent you briefly join a double track before peeling off to the right and climbing up on a single track. A couple of steep switchbacks lead you up onto an estate road/forest road where you climb up, passing the trail you just rode on your outbound loop. Within a few metres you're directed off to the left and you climb up slightly, running parallel to a fence with an opening round to your left. This

Single tracks in abundance

Roots are a common theme

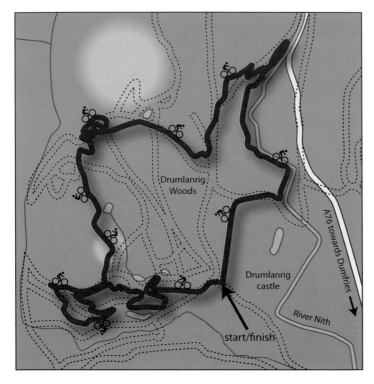

The single track switching down to the river

section continues for a few kilometres and climbs upwards: you will join on to a forest road and continue to climb up to a junction.

At the junction the trail climbs up through a series of single-track switchbacks into the trees. This section is quite tight and twisty and those of you with wide bars will have to take caution as some of the gaps between the trees are quite narrow. Once you cross the hill you will descend through a series of bermed corners and small jumps before a drop to your right takes you on to an estate road. Climbing up the estate road you have some fantastic views out to your left. Catch your breath and get ready for another tight single-track link across the top of the hill.

The next forest road section runs downhill. This is a fast descent and a shared trail so keep your eyes peeled for other trail users. You will also have to take a fork off to the left which drops you into a single-track trail. Take care when doing so as the trail narrows down significantly and passes over a ditch!

The next section of single track is very fast. Some of the corners tighten up on themselves so stay on your guard and cover those brakes. After

The return leg up the main drive to the castle

the single track you will climb on a very rough double track before forking off to your right and into more fast single tracks: take care further down this section as you will cross over a public road!

After the public road you have a few more kilometres of narrow single track. There is a short forest road link between sections and it provides a welcome break from the intense concentration required on the narrow trail. The lower part has some very tight turns to deal with and some sections of trail are quite exposed. There are also a few steep gradients and chunks of bedrock to deal with as you continue to descend down towards the river.

At the bottom of the descent you join a double track that runs parallel to the river. Here you have a chance to take a quick rest and enjoy the spectacular views of the river Nith before taking a right turn and climbing up through a series of steep and tight switchbacks. Traverse the hill on a single track and join into one of the estate roads for a few metres before entering the final section of single track, which drops back down towards the river. Once again you will join into a double track that leads you round to a white gate. Pass through the gate, making sure you shut it securely, and climb up onto the red tarmac drive. Taking a right turn climbing up on the tarmac back towards the castle and car park.

FIRE TOWER TRAIL

▶ FACILITIES

Car park and charges: Yes; charges apply

Cafe: No

Toilets: No

Showers: No

Bike wash: No

Nearest bike shop: Crinan Cycles, 34 Argyll Street, Lochgilphead, Argyll, PA31 8NE (01546 603 511)

Bike hire: Yes

Accommodation: B&Bs, hotels, self-catering accommodation and camping around the area. Most amenities in Lochgliphead.

Other trails on site: Natural trails, permissive paths and forest roads.

Ordnance Survey map: Explorer 358.

ENJOYMENT FOR SKILL LEVEL

Beginner: 5/10

Intermediate: 6/10

Advanced: 5/10

Getting there: Heading north from Lochgilphead on the A816 you will pass open ground and come into a right-hand corner with the B841 heading off to the left. As you exit the corner there is a forest road entrance on your right. The trailhead car park is located 1km up the forest road. You will pass some small industrial buildings on your right. Keep going straight on and you will see the car park on your right.

Grid ref: NR 85135 90837

Sat nav: PA31 8SJ

More info: www.forestry.gov.uk

▶ TRAIL 1

On-site grade: Red

Clive's grade: Blue with Red sections

Distance: 11.5km

Technicality: 5/10

Ascent: 366m

WHO IS THIS TRAIL GOOD FOR?

Beginner: 4/10

Intermediate: 6.5/10

Advanced: 5/10

Fire Tower trails

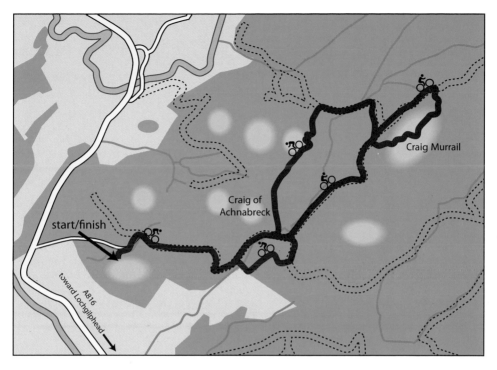

Craig Murrail

Craig of
Achnabreck

start/finish

toward Lochgilphead
A816

The Fire Tower trails are an exception among British trail centres. There is no specific loop as such here, just sections of Red trail that you can ride in any order you fancy and as many times as you want (there are multiple points at which you can enter the forest). There are waymarkers from the main car park that will lead you on an interesting loop. The layout comprises of a network of the single tracks and forest roads that are relatively easy to get your head around. I do, however, recommend following the signs for your first ride just to help you get your bearings.

From the car park head back out to the forest road that you drove in on. Take a right turn climbing up the hill. The forest road bears round to the right and in a few metres the gradient levels out as you crest the top of the hill. The forest road starts descending.

The first section of single track will come up in no time on your left-hand side. This is a very short section that traverses the hillside and will bring you back down to the forest road. Now you will head out into the forest and towards one of the first loops.

Narrow single track linked by forest roads

The short Black-option loop on the man hill is worth a look even if you walk up: the view is truly stunning

Just after a bridge take a left turn and continue to climb on the forest road. You will see your return section crossing from right to left as you climb on the main forest road. You will come to a fork in the trail, but keep right and continue to climb up the forest road. The gradient levels out and you will see a single-track trail on your right-hand side. This is the final section of climbing that leads you up to the summit cairn. As you twist your way up the hillside on single track you are rewarded for your efforts with some stunning views.

On top of the hill there is a Black-option line, a good challenge that climbs up onto the hilltop where you are presented with an absolutely stunning 360° panorama. The main trail then starts to descend. The trail is relatively narrow but the surface is smooth; it undulates and twists down through the trees with some open fast corners. At the bottom of this section you will join a forest road. Just before the forest road there is a Black-option line. This line involves a steep stone-pitched bank. Take care as at the time of riding the ground was quite soft and can easily stall the bike. The Red-trail option line is to the left. The gradient is easier but caution should still be taken as other forest users may be passing on the forest road below you.

When you join the forest road you will turn right then left and climb up slightly. The forest road then descends and once again you have a fantastic view as you traverse around the hillside. Here the signs become very vague – by a quarried edge you can take a left turn and shortcut to the main Murder Hill trail; if you continue further along the forest road you will get more single-track climbing to link to the same point. This single track switches its way up the hill, the surface is very natural and small rock outcrops are incorporated as technical features. The ride line becomes quite vague at times and you can tell that a lack of use is allowing nature to reclaim the trail.

From the top of the hill descend through a sweet series of switchbacks. Beyond these an open straight with lumps and bumps leads you down through the treeline to a forest road. Take a left turn on the forest road (you should recognise where you are at this point as you rode through this section on your outbound loop).

Head straight on up the forest road until you see a single track to your right. This trail will traverse the hillside before dropping down through a series of bermed corners to a ford. When the river is in spate the water here can be very deep and fast running, so it's best left for the drier months. After the ford you climb up a steep bank to a forest road. Take a left turn and return back to the car park by following this main forest road. Of course, if you're not ready to head back you have the option of heading out and taking in any one of the loops again.

A short yet fun descent from Murder Hill

The ford can become very deep with fast-flowing water, and it's best to avoid this section in wetter periods

FORT WILLIAM – NEVIS RANGE

FACILITIES

Car park and charges: Yes; charges apply

Cafe: Yes

Toilets: Yes

Showers: No

Bike wash: Yes

Nearest bike shop: On site

Bike hire: Yes

Accommodation: B&Bs, hotels, self-catering accommodation and camping around the area. All amenities in nearby Fort William.

Other trails on site: World Cup Downhill, Red downhill, 4X, skills area, Red "Ten Under The Ben" loop.

Ordnance Survey map: Explorer 392.

ENJOYMENT FOR SKILL LEVEL

Beginner: 3/10

Intermediate: 7.5/10

Advanced: 9.5/10

Getting there: The trailhead is located at the Nevis range lift station. Following the A82 north-east from Fort William, pass the village of Torlundy. Just over a kilometre past Torlundy turn right and follow the signs to the Nevis range ski centre. Approaching from the north following the A82 from Speen Bridge, you will see the signs for the ski centre indicating a left turn up a side road.

Grid ref: NN 17209 77440

Sat nav: PA31 8SJ

More info: www.nevisrange.co.uk

▶**TRAIL 1: BROOMSTICK BLUE**

On-site grade: Blue

Clive's grade: Green with Blue sections

Distance: 7km

Technicality: 3/10

Ascent: 125m

ENJOYMENT FOR SKILL LEVEL

Beginner: 6/10

Intermediate: 6.5/10

Advanced: 4/10

From the car park the Blue route starts by heading out on the road that you drove in on. The road is wider and visibility is good. You only follow the road for several hundred metres before turning left up some steps and through a fence where you join a gravel track.

This gravel double track blends into a disused tarmac road. The speed is quite high as you descend following the river down towards the village of Torlundy. Just before the village take a left turn and head down to the North Face car park. From here it's mainly single track the whole way back up to the Nevis range car park, and throughout this section you'll be running parallel to a river on your right. There are a few boardwalk sections but they're relatively wide and short.

After 1km you will run parallel to a dry stone wall with open ground to your left. Here the trail joins in to a shared user trail. Please be aware of other trail users: this

Smooth, easy-going trail on the Blue route

section can get quite fast in paces as you drop down to a bridge crossing over the river. The final section leading back to the car park is a little more undulating and again you may come across other trail users

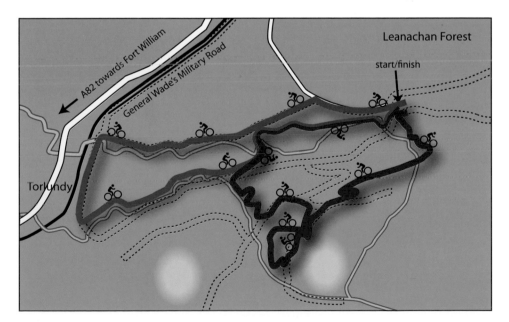

as this is where the high-wire experience is located.

▶ TRAIL 2: WORLD CHAMPS XC

On-site grade: Red

Clive's grade: Red

Distance: 7.7km

Technicality: 6.5/10

Ascent: 269m

ENJOYMENT FOR SKILL LEVEL

Beginner: 2/10

Intermediate: 6.5/10

Advanced: 7.5/10

Starting from the car park look for the two posts marked 'World Champs Trail'. You climb up next to the 4X track where the signs become vague (just after the initial short steep bank), you will see a boardwalk to your right and this links you to a piece of gravel single-track trail on the far side.

Avoid the temptation to ride straight on past the boardwalk as this will just access the 4X track.

After the boardwalk a single track twists through tight trees. You will pass through a large pipe and the trail climbs steeply on the exit to the pipe. After a short section of single track you will come out of the trees and climb up next to a forest road. The trail then blends into the forest road and climbs up to a junction where you take a right turn. Take care through this section as you will have riders coming down towards you from the Red downhill trail!

The forest road is quite rough and loose so you have to work hard to find traction. At the top, bear right into a double track. Here the trail goes over a beautifully built wooden bridge. Be careful: this section is a shared trail and you may encounter other trail users heading in the opposite direction.

You will come to a fork in the trail where you turn left and start climbing up. The trail switchbacks and heads up into the trees. The gradient gets quite steep in places here, especially the final ramp that leads you

The opening boardwalk with skinny option

The return trail passes over the large pipe. Head straight on up the forest road

The first descent switches down the hill

up to a forest road. Turning right onto the forest road, continue to climb upwards. You will see the bridge made from a large pipe to pass through as you go under the return route crossing point. Continue to climb up the forest road and take a left into more single track just before a large metal gate. A few more metres of climbing and you are at the top of the hill with spectacular views.

A brief moment here to catch a breath before descending through a series of switchbacks and rock drops passing over the bridge (crossing the forest roads that you just climbed on). Throughout this section of single track you have some cheeky rock drops and multiple tight and loose rocky corners. The descent is split up into sections with a forest road link, some sections of the trail are quite rough and those of you riding hard-tails will have to be careful on the sharp rocks.

The final section takes you back down to the river where you join in with the Blue trail for a few hundred metres back to the car park. The World Cup trail follows the boundary of the car park before turning right, climbing up a short sharp forest road and into a final section of single track that drops you back down to the edge of the car park, where you started the trail.

The return to the car park is shared with the Blue trail

▶ DOWNHILL TRAILS

Clive's grade: Black, Red

Distance: N/A

Technicality: 10/10

ENJOYMENT FOR SKILL LEVEL

Beginner: 0/10

Intermediate: 5/10

Advanced: 9.5/10

The main downhill trail at Fort William is world-class. It has been host to World Cup race events for the last decade and hosted the 2007 World Championships. With the main racetrack running below the gondola, the track is very demanding and is only really suitable for riders with a high level of experience in similar terrain. The speeds are high and the surfaces are very rough, there are also some large jumps that you have to commit to and plenty of rock drops.

The Red trail comprises of single-track sections, boardwalk and bedrock. There are a few steep gradients in the trail as well as the obligatory jumps and drops to deal with. The opening sections of the trail are made up of a long boardwalk. There is quite a high level of exposure of the side of the raised wooden trail and may not be to everyone's taste. Once again, this isn't a trail for the faint-hearted and even though it is graded Red it is more like a Black-graded cross-country trail.

Make sure you have the appropriate equipment including gloves, full-face helmets, body armour (including spine board), goggles/glasses and it's vital that your bike is suitable for the task. Your bike should be in top working order as the rigors of the downhill tracks will put a lot of strain on both you and your bike.

Rock drops at the finish of the downhill trails

GLENTRESS

The new bike shop and cafe at Glentress

▶ FACILITIES

Car park and charges: Yes; charges apply

Cafe: Yes

Toilets: Yes

Showers: Yes

Bike wash: Yes

Nearest bike shop: On site

Bike hire: Yes

Accommodation: B&Bs, Hotels, camping and self-catering accommodation in and around the Tweed Valley area.

Other trails on site: Green, Black, Orange freeride park and skills area, permissive paths and forest roads.

Ordnance Survey map: Explorer 337.

ENJOYMENT FOR SKILL LEVEL

Beginner: 9/10

Intermediate: 10/10

Advanced: 9/10

Getting there: From Edinburgh take the A703 to Peebles, turn left at the roundabout in Peebles and head east on the A72 towards Galashiels. You will see Glentress Forest on your left.

Grid ref: NT 28522 39867

Sat nav: EH45 8NB

More info: www.forestry.gov.uk www.7stanesmountainbiking.com

▶ TRAIL 1: RED

On-site grade: Red

Clive's grade: Red

Distance: 18km

Technicality: 8/10

Ascent: 585m

ENJOYMENT FOR SKILL LEVEL

Beginner: 5/10

Intermediate: 7/10

Advanced: 8/10

From the newly built Peel Centre follow the trail signs past the shop and cafe and on to the forest road. You will climb on the forest road for a few metres. Take care on this section as this is the main access road to the upper Buzzard's Nest car park and you may encounter vehicles.

You will bear right onto a quieter forest track and continue to climb slightly before taking a left into the first section of single track. This section of trail is shared with the Green and Blue routes. Within this opening section of single track you have a few option lines clearly signed.

Join a section of forest road near Squirrels car park, continue to climb before taking a left turn and into another single-track climb. This section winds its way up

All trails share the first climb

the hillside through large pines and there are a few little ramps that require some effort as you climb higher and higher above the Tweed Valley.

This section of trail is quite long and there are a couple of crossing points for the return Blue trail. Visibility is good but do keep an eye out to your left up the hillside for descending riders. In the upper part of this section before the next forest road crossing you have the option of a few low-level skinny log rides. This area of hillside is a great place to practise some skills before heading on to the main trails.

After you cross the forest road the gradient levels out and you climb through some younger pines. Once again you have a few skinny long ride options but there is nothing too challenging within this section. When you leave the small pines behind, you come out into the open and the trail takes in a few more switchbacks.

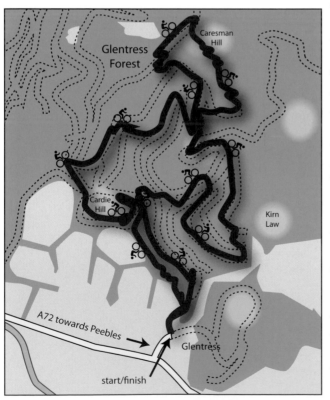

Skinny log rides in the opening climb give you a chance to hone your skills

Once again you are presented with some option lines of various grades. This single-track trail runs up above the main forest road and will link you to the Buzzard's Nest car park. As this is the main car park for the jump and skills areas, it can get quite busy here so take care when crossing the car park!

Continue straight on and around the metal gate, climbing upwards on a forest road. The skills areas will be to your right as you climb up. Take a right turn and pass the top of the jump park/skills area.

The Red route continues along forest road (you will see the Blue trail cross from left to right). A few hundred metres past the skills area you drop into a nice section of single track to your right. Throughout this section you encounter some tight switch-backs, small jumps, stream crossings, and some slightly steeper rougher sections.

The downhill section is short-lived and you're soon into another single-track line traversing its way up the hillside through a

series of switchbacks. This then joins an old forest road, giving you a chance to grab a breath and enjoy the view down the valley before climbing up to your left on single track.

Once again you encounter tight switch-backs. These ones are steeper and require a bit more effort than the last section. The trail levels out and you traverse to a forest road taking a tight left and climbing upwards. This can catch you out if you've not preselected the correct gear.

The forest road climbs up and you have a wonderful view back down the valley to your left as you traverse around the hillside. You will see the last climb just down below you. After several hundred metres the trail turns off to the right and climbs up a steep hillside on single track. Once again you will encounter tight switchbacks and some steeper gradients.

At the top of the single-track climb you come out into the open and will join a forest road taking a right turn climbing up

The Tweed valley, classic Scottish scenery

towards Spooky Woods. Near the top of this section just after you come into the treeline the gradient starts to steepen up. This only lasts for approximately 150m before you turn right into a single track.

The next section is named Spooky Woods, which comprises of tabletop jumps, double jumps, rock drops, flowing berm corners, and a bomb hole thrown in for good measure. This section of trail is a firm favourite among visitors to the forest and is built in a more modern trail-centre style compared to the rest of the descent. At the end of Spooky Woods, cross a forest road, rejoin the old Red route and descend downhill on a trail that is much narrower and rougher.

The single track eventually joins an old forest road and levels out. Continue on the forest road and blend to a wider, more established forest road. Climb up for a few metres. The trail leaves the forest road and drops down to your left. This is a relatively uneventful section, however there is a tight left-hand switchback in the lower part of this trail that is quite loose so don't let your guard down.

There are two sections of single track before the final descent. These are split by a short section of forest road. Take care when climbing on the forest road as there may be vehicles heading both up and down.

You will turn off left into the final descent, which comprises of fast-flowing single track, tight rough corners and drops. The initial part of the section is quite smooth and fast. After a short rise the trail narrows down and becomes quite rough in places.

After an open section you switch tight right into the trees. Here there is a split-line option, keep left for the Red trail or turn right for the Black option. At the bottom of the descent you will run along next to a fence and a pinch gap slows you down before joining the forest road, head back down to the Peel Centre and car parks.

▶ TRAIL 2: BLUE

On-site grade: Blue

Clive's grade: Blue

Distance: 13km

Technicality: 3/10

Ascent: 325m

ENJOYMENT FOR SKILL LEVEL

Beginner: 8.5/10

Intermediate: 9/10

Advanced: 3/10

The Blue trail heads out up the same route as the previous Red trail. When you arrive at the top in the Buzzard's Nest car park the signs become slightly vague. The Blue trail drops down a small gully from the top right-hand corner of the car park; you need to go straight ahead across the car park and turn right. Here you should see the gully and the trail straight ahead of you, take care as the Blue trail crosses from left to right on its return leg.

Following the outbound loop descend slightly before you climb up. This section is shared with the Red and the next stage linking up to the forest road could be considered quite tough for a Blue-graded trail. At the time of writing there was a

diversion and unfortunately we could not ride the upper loop. The diversion took a left turn of the forest road on the Blue return: this is a fast descent linking into a single-track climb,

When you get to the top of the short climb, descend slightly on a forest road before turning right into Blue Velvet. This is a lovely flowing piece of single track with an easy rolling surface.

After crossing the forest road through a pinch fence, join into Berm Baby Berm, a smooth fast trail with movement and basic features that snakes down the hillside back towards Buzzard's Nest car park.

At the end of this section you cross over the Blue outbound trail and head straight on past the car park to your right and into

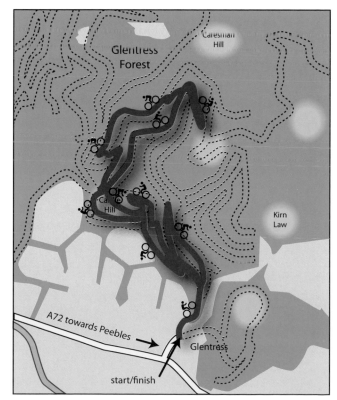

more flowing trail dropping back down to the main forest road.

After you cross the forest road you are in the final sections of downhill and you will have option lines to take rock drops, whoops and jumps. You will cross the outbound climb partway down so keep an eye out down to your right for riders below you. A series of switchbacks drops you onto a forest road. A slight descent heads back towards the Peel Centre. One final section of trail links to another forest road and you're homeward bound.

▶ALSO WORTH RIDING

ARRAN

Cross-country trails, Castle Blue 10km, Blue 10km, Red 18km and 35km Black trail

Camping, hotels and B&Bs in the area

Location: From the west coast of Scotland there are two ferries that go to Arran: Ardrossan to Brodick and Claonaig to Lochranza. For the Ardrossan to Brodick crossing take the M77 from Glasgow to Kilmarnock (or A71 from M74 junction 8), then take the A71 towards Irving where you need to pick up the A78 coast road and head north to Saltcoats. You will see signs to the harbour from here.

Grid ref: NR 96164 36042

Sat nav: Arran

Info: www.arranbikeclub.com

CARRON VALLEY

Cross country trail, Red-grade loop with Orange freeride line

Camping, hotels and B&Bs in the area

Location: From the main A872 in Denny pick up the B818 sign posted to Fintry. After approximately 6km on the B818 you will pass through Carron Bridge, the car park is on your left 2km beyond the village.

Grid ref: NS 76038 83763

Sat nav: Carron Bridge, Falkirk FK6

Info: www.forestry.gov.uk

LEARNIE RED ROCK TRAIL

Cross-country trails, Green, Blue and Black-grade trails with jump spots

Camping, hotels and B&Bs in the area

Location: Head North on the A9 to the Tore roundabout with the A832. From the roundabout leave the A9 and head towards Cromarty on the A832, pass through Rosemarkie and after approximately 5km you will see the car park on your right.

Grid ref: NH 736614

Sat nav: Rosemarkie

Info: www.forestry.gov.uk

GLENTROOL

▶ FACILITIES

Car park and charges: Yes; charges apply

Cafe: Yes

Toilets: Yes

Showers: No

Bike wash: No

Nearest bike shop: On site at Kirroughtree forest

Bike hire: Yes from Kirroughtree

Accommodation: B&Bs, hotels, self-catering accommodation and camping around the area. All amenities in nearby Newton Stewart.

Other trails on site: Purple, Green, permissive paths and forest roads.

Ordnance Survey map: Explorer 319.

ENJOYMENT FOR SKILL LEVEL

Beginner: 9/10

Intermediate: 7/10

Advanced: 4/10

Getting there: From the A75 trunk road, turn off at Newton Stewart and head north on the A714 for approximately 13km. You will see signs directing you right to Glentrool village. Pass the village and you will pick up signs to the forest car park.

The trails start by the cafe.

Grid ref: NX 37181 78587

Sat nav: Glentrool

More info: www.7stanesmountainbiking.com

▶ TRAIL 1

On-site grade: Blue

Clive's grade: Blue

Distance: 9.2km

Technicality: 4/10

Ascent: 192m

ENJOYMENT FOR SKILL LEVEL

Beginner: 9/10

Intermediate: 10/10

Advanced: 4/10

Glentrool trail information is located just above the cafe

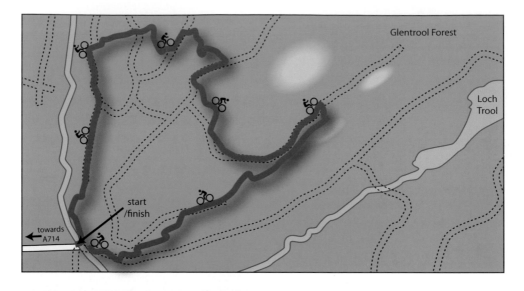

The trail heads out up a small rise next to the cafe. Here the surface is smooth and the trail is relatively wide. You'll pass over a small bridge before climbing up slightly. The gradient is reasonably mellow but the climb does go on for a few kilometres.

The trail joins into a forest road where you continue straight ahead up to a fork. Keep left and continue to follow the forest road. You will come to the first section of single track that traverses open ground. The surface is smooth and the going relatively easy.

A forest road link puts you into another section of single track. Once again traversing open ground, you will take a right turn onto a forest road that descends down before forking off to the left into another section of single track. The single track eventually joins back into the forest road and you have some spectacular views out to your right up towards Loch Trool.

The outbound trail

Great views at the top of the Blue trail

Taking the switchback right, the trail climbs up on single track to the summit of a small knoll. This is the start of the final descent. Throughout the descent you will find plenty of fast corners and some sizeable bermed corners. The surface is smooth but get off the ride line and you're into some loose shale.

The single-track trail crosses over a forest road then continues to descend through the treeline. A forest road link brings you back to the far end of the car park where you started the loop.

Narrow, fast single track leads you back down to the cafe and car parks

GOLSPIE

►FACILITIES

Car park and charges: Yes; donations in the pot go towards ongoing trail work

Cafe: No

Toilets: No

Showers: No

Bike wash: No

(Toilets and parking available in Golspie town centre just below the trailhead car park)

Nearest bike shop: There may be cycle shops closer but your best bet is to head 80km south to Inverness for a well-stocked specialist

Bike hire: None on site

Accommodation: Accommodation available in varying forms around the area; the nearby town of Golspie has most amenities. The larger towns of Brora in the north and Dornoch in the south have a wider variety of facilities and amenities.

Other trails on site: Black, natural permissive paths and forest roads.

Ordnance Survey map: Explorer 441.

ENJOYMENT FOR SKILL LEVEL

Beginner: 3/10

Intermediate: 7/10

Advanced: 8/10

Getting there: Golspie is located on the A9 between Dornoch and Brora. You can park in the town just below the church or further up the lane there is a specific car park. From the south enter the town of Golspie and follow the main road round to the right. Bear to your left, and along the seafront there will be a car park and the toilet block. You can either park here or continue straight on up the lane past the monument and underneath the railway to the trailhead car park on your right.

Grid ref: NC 83012 00329

Sat nav: Golspie

More info: www.highlandwildcat.com

►WILD CAT TRAIL

On-site grade: Red

Clive's grade: Red

Distance: 7km

Technicality: 6/10

Ascent: 247m

ENJOYMENT FOR SKILL LEVEL

Beginner: 3/10

Intermediate: 7/10

Advanced: 7/10

Both the Red and Black trails start at the same location in the lower corner of the car park. The opening section of trail has an introduction to the rock slabs and boulders that you'll find in the final descent. There are a couple of option lines here and it's a good place to start the day and get warmed up before going into the first climb.

The climb switches its way up the hillside on a nice easy-going piece of single track. Partway the single track is broken with a very short section of double track. Signage is good so you should have no problems finding your way.

You will pass over a cattle grid between a large fence while you're in the single track. Just beyond this you take a right turn. Here the gradient levels out and you will have a large deer fence to your right. You only just get a chance to catch your breath before taking a left turn into single track. Start to climb once more, but be wary not to miss this left turn as the foliage hides the entrance.

Your parking contributions go back into the upkeep of the trails

The next section of trail is relatively easy as you switch around the hillside, giving you a chance to look back down to the coastline and appreciate the spectacular views. You will eventually arrive at a forest road where the Red trail turns left. The Black trail goes straight ahead and continues in a similar vein to the section you've just been riding.

Option lines at the start give you a taster of what's to come

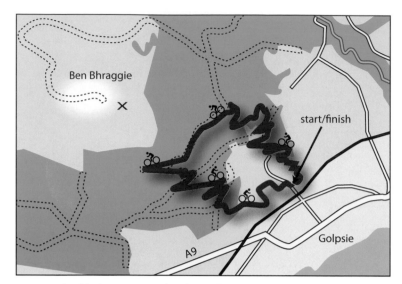

signposted to take a forest road climb on your right. The forest road narrows into a double track and you climb up with open ground up to your right. You will come to a turning circle where on your right-hand side you are rejoined by the Black trail.

The descent has multiple technical features. Some of the jumps are made from large rocks, some are double jumps and other large pieces of stone act as fly-off jumps. There are many bermed corners throughout the lower section and the surface is relatively good although slightly rough in places.

I highly recommend riding this section: at the top you can cut across to the large monument and avoid a boring open hilltop section.

As you will see in the images, at the time of riding we were dealing with some snow and the decision was made to stay low and push on, rather than spending all day pushing the bike, and get another Scottish trail ticked off of our list.

The Red trail continues down the forest road and after a short distance you will be

When you arrive at the bottom of the descent a series of medium-sized tabletops lead you out into the open and there is the option of a log ride to your right. The last section of trail runs round a field back to the country lane and car park.

Technical rock sections are that bit more challenging in the snow

INNERLEITHEN

▶ FACILITIES

Car park and charges: Yes; charges apply

Cafe: No

Toilets: Yes

Showers: No

Bike wash: No

Nearest bike shop: I-Cycles, 4 Traquair Road, Innerleithen, Peebleshire, EH44 6PD (01896 833848)

Bike hire: Alpine Bikes, Neidpath Church Building, Peebles Road, Innerleithen, EH44 6QX (01896 830880)

Accommodation: B&Bs, hotels, camping and self-catering accommodation in and around the Tweed Valley area.

Other trails on site: Downhill tracks, permissive paths and forest tracks.

Ordnance Survey map: Explorer 337.

ENJOYMENT FOR SKILL LEVEL

Beginner: 3/10

Intermediate: 6/10

Advanced: 10/10

Getting there: From Edinburgh, take the A703 to Peebles. Turn left at the roundabout in Peebles and head east on the A72 towards Galashiels. You will pass Glentress Forest on your left. When you come in to Innerleithen, take a right turn just after the Co-Op sign posted to the trails. The car park is just out of town over the bridge on your left.

Grid ref: NT 33584 35809

Sat nav: EH44 6PD

More info: www.7stanesmountainbiking.com; www.upliftscotland.com

▶ TRAIL 1

On-site grade: Red

Clive's grade: Red with Black sections

Distance: 18.5km

Technicality: 8/10

Ascent: 585m

ENJOYMENT FOR SKILL LEVEL

Beginner: 3/10

Intermediate: 6.5/10

Advanced: 9/10

Take care on the shared sections of trail

Innerleithen has been home to mountain bike race events for years. It's hosted national championships and regional races for over two decades. The hill has also featured in many DVDs and regular uplifts provide all important practice time to enthusiastic racers and amateurs alike.

The Red XC trail has to be one of the toughest of the 7stanes mountain bike trails. The trail is a simple climb up to the top of Minch Moor and return via a long descent with short bits of climbing and traversing.

From the car park, follow the outbound trail, crossing over the country lane and turning right, then climbing up next to a fence. Be careful as this area gets very busy: this is where the downhill trails all finish. You will switchback up the hillside with fields to your right. The gradient here is quite steep and there is no easy way other than walking to deal with this section of trail.

The gradient on the first climb is quite steep and sustained

Up in the treeline the trail levels out and follows a double track that continues to climb. After approximately 500m you will leave the double track and turn left into a single-track trail that climbs up and switches its way around the hillside. Throughout this section you will encounter rocks in the trail that you have to ride up onto and over. Many of these now have desire lines

The river Tweed below the main hill

around them, which you can opt for if you feel the gradient is too challenging.

You will join a forest road, taking a right then taking a slight descent before branching off to the left and climbing on more single track. Further along this section of trail you will descend ever so slightly – don't be fooled into thinking the climb is over as you will soon be back into the world of burning thighs. Partway up the climb you will come across a disused quarry. Here the trail drops through a series of switchbacks into the quarry. The surface here is a very rough and loose.

The exit to the quarry section has various option lines, all of which are quite steep and will bring you out on a forest road. When you join the forest road take a left turn and continue to climb upwards. This forest road comes out into the open and traverses around the hillside – you will have wonderful views out to your right. This section leads you to the next piece of single track which will be on your left-hand side. You will pass over an old dry stone wall as you enter this section of trail. Beyond the wall get ready for technical rock sections and plenty more climbing.

Throughout this next section you will cross over a forest road and

at a right-hand switchback you have the option to take a shortcut, missing out the top of the hill. This can be advisable on very windy days.

Beyond the right-hand switchback the trail will eventually come out into the open as you traverse across Minch Moor. The gradient up here is not as bad as the start of the climb and you will arrive at the summit cairn in no time. On a clear day, the views up here are spectacular: you have a 360° panorama of the Scottish Borders.

You will now begin to descend the open hillside. The initial part of the downhill has a smooth surface but in some of the corners it can get quite loose. The first section of

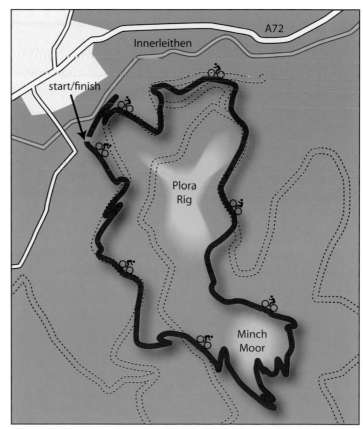

the downhill is pretty uneventful and will lead you to the Southern Upland Way. Cross the Southern Upland Way and drop into a newly built section. Throughout this section of trail you will come cross rocky drops, jumps and bermed corners. Some of these features you really have to work for and others you will seem to float over with little effort.

This section links into a narrow single-track trail. The trees here have recently been clear-felled and this has dramatically changed the overall feel of this section. The trail levels out before you start to descend down towards a forest road, Take care through this section as the speed is quite high and there is a wooden pinch fence to slow you down onto the forest road.

Turn left onto the forest road and traverse around the hillside, dropping down and climbing up slightly. The next section of single track will be on your right-hand side. This is a fantastic piece of trail with great features. There are some good technical rock sections and if you fancy an even greater challenge partway down you can take a right turn and join a Black-graded section.

Both the Red and Black trails are rough and feel very natural. The lower part of this descent is bench cut into the hillside and you will have to navigate multiple rock drops and switchback turns. The trail then starts to climb uphill slightly and will join a forest road. Take care on the weekends as this forest road is used to uplift the downhill riders so you may come across vehicles.

Follow the forest road straight on, passing a large quarry on your left and traverse around the hillside, climbing up slightly. You will arrive at the top of the last descent clearly marked with good signage and large rocks.

The final descent offers lots of opportunity to catch some airtime

Looking down to town at the start of Caddon Bank

This section of trail, named Caddon Bank, really does push the grade into the next level. Full of large rock drops, the surface is loose and there are many blind crests to deal with. You will also find that the speed is quite high in places.

In the lower sections of the downhill there are some great opportunities to catch some air with step-downs, doubles and tabletop jumps. The final switchbacks are quite tight and are a good indicator that your descent is over. Simply cross back over the country lane and roll into the car park.

▶DOWNHILL TRAILS

Clive's grade: Orange/Black

Distance: N/A

Technicality: 9/10

ENJOYMENT FOR SKILL LEVEL

Beginner: 3/10

Intermediate: 7/10

Advanced: 10/10

There are four permanent downhill tracks at Innerleithen. All of these trails have been specifically built for downhill and long travel suspension bikes. If you decide to ride them, prepare for off camber, large roots, rock gardens, drop-offs, double jumps, tabletops and a variety of trail surfaces. There is an uplift service that runs most weekends throughout the spring, summer and autumn. More information can be found at www.upliftscotland.com.

Narrow, tight and technically challenging trails for downhill and all mountain bikes

KIRROUGHTREE

▶ FACILITIES

Car park and charges: Yes; charges apply

Cafe: Yes

Toilets: Yes

Showers: No

Bike wash: Yes

Nearest bike shop: On site

Bike hire: Yes

Accommodation: B&Bs, hotels, self-catering accommodation and camping around the area. All amenities are in nearby Newton Stewart or back along the A75 at Creetown and further east at Castle Douglas.

Other trails on site: Green, Blue, Red, permissive paths and forest tracks.

Ordnance Survey map: Explorer 319.

ENJOYMENT FOR SKILL LEVEL

Beginner: 9/10

Intermediate: 9/10

Advanced: 8/10

Getting there: Kirroughtree Forest is located in south-west Scotland near the village of Stronord on the north side of the A75, just under 5km past Creetown.

Grid ref: NX 45167 64815

Sat nav: Newton Stewart, Creetown or Stronord

More info: www.7stanesmountainbiking.com

▶ TRAIL 1: LARG HILL

On-site grade: Blue

Clive's grade: Blue

Distance: 9.5km

Technicality: 6/10

Ascent: 200m

ENJOYMENT FOR SKILL LEVEL

Beginner: 6.5/10

Intermediate: 10/10

Advanced: 4/10

All the outbound trails start at the same point by the trailhead signage. The initial section of single-track switchbacks up through the trees next to the skills loop on your right. You will come out on a forest road where you take a right turn and continue to climb for a few more metres before taking a left into a single-track climb. The gradient is quite steep for the grade of trail and some of the switchbacks you may find tight.

The trail levels out and after another sequence of switchbacks joins on to an old forest road. Continue to climb upwards on the forest road, blending in to a larger smoother forest road where you descend slightly and bear round to the right at a

T-Junction. The forest road splits and you need to keep to the left-hand side, climbing up slightly as you do so. You will then enter a single track through a gap in a dry stone wall on your right.

Once again you will switchback up a small hill, crossing the forest road and into the next section of single track. Here you have the split line for the Blue to your left and the Red trail heading outwards on your right. Take a left turn and descend on a nice fast section of single track, the surface is smooth although if you get off the ride line you'll find it's quite loose. You will then cross over a forest road and into another section of single track. Here there are some really nice fast corners and some good movement to the trail.

When you exit the single track, join on to a forest road. This traverses around the hill

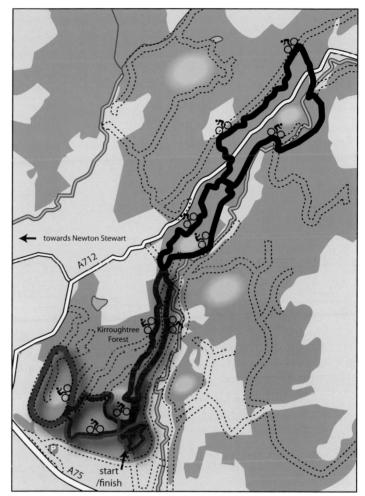

for a few hundred metres before turning right. Continue to climb uphill on forest roads. You will come to a turning circle and to your right-hand side a steep slab where the Red trail drops down.

Both the Blue and the Red trails head down the next section of single track to your left, this starts between two large boulders. The surface throughout this section can get quite rough and really does push the limit of the Blue grade. Cross over a forest road and into another short section

of single track before blending back onto the forest road and descending slightly. The signs are great on all 7stanes trails and you'll have no issue in finding your way.

A short single-track link drops down to another forest road where you take a left turn and continue to descend. After a few hundred metres, you will turn right into another section of single track. This trail dips down and climbs up. There are a few interesting technical features to deal with including jumps, rock drops, and tight

Mrs Forth enjoys the fast single-track descent

corners. You will also pass a small loch to your right. This is where the Stane for this centre can be found.

At the end of this section you will drop onto a forest road. The Red route takes a left turn and climbs up the forest road. To complete the Blue loop head straight over into the next section of single track. Partway down this section the Red trail will rejoin from the left so keep an eye out for riders. Visibility is good here so you should have no problems.

The last section of trail will hopefully put a big smile on your face. A series of fast corners traverse around the hillside as you descend back towards the fields and the visitor centre. There are a couple of split-line options throughout this section, one of which drops through quite a tight and sizeable bomb hole. There is an alternative line to the left around this – take care as the entrance to it is blind!

When you exit the trees you'll be on an old double track. Climb up the hill, traversing between pine trees, before a right-hand corner leads you down a fast ramp to the back of the visitor centre.

▶TRAIL 2: BLACK CRAIGS

On-site grade: Red & Black

Clive's grade: Red for the Red sections and Black for the far loop

Distance: 31.2km

Technicality: 8/10

Ascent: 762m

ENJOYMENT FOR SKILL LEVEL

Beginner: 1/10

Intermediate: 5/10

Advanced: 9/10

The Black Craigs route heads out on the same outbound trail as the Blue and Red trails. After a forest road crossing you arrive at a fork in the trail where the Red trail heads right and the Blue left. Take a right turn and climb up some steep gradients through switchbacks heading into the trees.

The single track continues to traverse the hillside with some tight corners and good movement. The trail surface is relatively smooth, although there are a few outcrops of rock you have to drop down or ride over. Partway through the section you will have a split-line option: the more challenging of the two lines is to your right and will drop down a series of boulders and bedrock linking you back on to the stone-built trail. At the end of the section there is another split-line option: to your left is a blind crest that rolls into a steep rock slab and to the right is an easy Red-graded version that drops down around the large rock outcrop.

Cross over the forest road into a single track heading downhill. There is a small rise in the trail and quite a rough stone-pitched section. At the end you will cross over a forest road. Continue to follow the shared trail on more single track. The single track blends into a forest road and you descend slightly before taking a right turn and down a short single-track link to another forest road where you take a left turn.

Follow the forest road for a short distance before turning off to the right into another section of single track. Through this section there are a couple of rock-drop-option lines and some tight corners with blind crests. At the end of this section of trail you will join on to a forest road where you start to climb up.

At the top of the short forest road climb you will see the anniversary cairn on your right. Here you have some spectacular views of the hills. Just beyond the cairn you branch off to the left. Heading into more single track, you will climb up for a short distance and have a series of tight switchbacks to deal with.

The single-track trail continues to traverse across the hillside and a cheeky rock garden leads you into a set of uphill switchbacks. After the short climb the trail drops

The stone-pitched section in the first descent requires top technique

Classic Kirroughtree single track – you're kept busy while climbing

down over a series of rocky outcrops and stone-pitching. Desire lines have appeared predominantly to the right of the main ride line.

You will eventually arrive at another forest road crossing, beyond which you enter a section known as The Nutcracker, another classic piece of Kirroughtree single track. Most of the sections here have names that are marked on the blue posts. Traverse the hillside and a short descent links you to The White Witch.

This section of trail runs parallel to a country lane and climbs up slightly as it does so. You will join the country lane for a few metres heading northwards before turning right into Rivendell. It should be noted that if you needed to take a short cut back for any reason you can do so by taking a right turn and following the country lane. This is marked on the blue post.

Rivendell is a fun but short descent, comprising of switchbacks, blind crests, rock drops and plenty of fast corners that drop-down the hillside before joining into a forest road. At this point the Black trail heads out to the left and the Red trail returns to the right.

You will now follow forest road for just over 1km with the river down to your right. At a forest road junction head straight on then turn left into a single-track trail. This section is named Stairway to Heaven. This is quite a tough climb and you will find some steep gradients and tight switchbacks as you climb up the hillside. There is also a tight right turn onto an exposed section of bedrock that poses a good challenge and will test even the best riders.

When you get to the top of the hill, switchback round and start to traverse

the hillside before a good descent leads you back down to the river. The speed on the descent is quite high in places and some of the corners tighten up; there are the inevitable blind crests to deal with. At the bottom of the descent you take a hard switch right, dropping down into a left turn onto the forest road.

A short forest road link leads to another section of single track named The Troglodyte. This short section runs parallel to the forest road, which you will rejoin before crossing over the river and taking a left turn heading out towards McMoab.

A kilometre of gentle climbing leads you up to McMoab. This section of trail can be avoided by simply continuing along the forest road. McMoab is 90% bedrock – there

Stone-pitched sections in the downhills split up the smooth trail surface

are blue painted arrows on the rock that will help you navigate your way through the undulating bedrock. This section of trail is quite physically demanding and you have to keep your wits about you as it is easy to be led astray from the mainline. You will drop off a large spine of bedrock and back onto a stone trail with the river running parallel to your left. A short climb leads you out of McMoab back to the forest road. At the end of the section there is an option line to your right. This leads you to a large rock slab that drops onto the forest road; alternatively you can turn left and take a smaller drop joining on to the forest road.

The open bedrock granite of McMoab offers multiple ride lines

The trail then heads up towards the main Queens Way Road (A712), crossing over a river and climbing slightly with open ground on your right. Take a left turn onto the A712 and after a few metres you'll see a sign right onto Heartbreak Hill. The Heartbreak Hill section climbs up the hillside. The gradient here is reasonably steep, and it's for this reason that it's sometimes worth taking a shortcut past McMoab and saving the energy to make light work of this hill. You will join on to a forest road and climb up for a few more metres, there is still some more climbing to do before you reach the summit of Black Craigs at 237 m.

The single-track trail switches up the hillside with some steep gradients and tight corners. At the summit cairn you start to descend, traversing the top of the ridge line above the Queensway. Expect to encounter some tight corners, rock drops, and superb sections of trail that will keep you on your toes. This long traverse and descent will eventually bring you back down to the A712.

Rocky sections require total commitment, especially in the wet

Cross over the main road and a short single track links to a forest road. This starts to climb and you will see signs that point you to the right into a section of single track. The obligatory tight switchbacks and steep gradients traverse through a section named Hansel and Gretel, before leading you up to a forest road crossing and into Hissing Sid. This section of trail gets very rough in places and you will come across a few large bedrock sections that require a high level of skill to navigate through.

After this fine section of single track you will arrive back at the country lane. The trail runs parallel to the lane for a few metres before joining on to the public road and taking a left turn. This short section is named Jabberwocky and a rough steep descent drops you back down to rejoin into the Red trail. There are a few cheeky rock drops in this section and some tight corners, the surface can become quite slippery in the wet!

The final section of the descent is shared with the Red. A series of switchbacks leads you down to the forest road that runs parallel with the river. The forest road bears round to the right and climbs up the hill back to the country lane. You will rejoin the lane here and ride along a country lane for a few metres before taking a right turn, climbing up through switchbacks on single-track trail.

There are still a few kilometres to go before you're back to the visitor centre, and this single track can really sap your energy as you dip down and climb up several times throughout the remainder of the loop. Cross over a forest road into

a series of tight switchbacks up to a steep gradient and into another short descent. Within a few metres of the descent there is a split line and an easier Red Line heads off to your right. The Black option takes a left, climbing up over a series of bedrock sections. Preceding one short climb there is a rock slab drop, nothing too major but the set-up can be quite tricky as you climb a short steep gradient and have to turn left into the slab drop.

The two trails converge and continue to traverse the hillside. There are a few exposed sections on this trail and a couple of rock drops that require some attention. After a small rise in large pines the trail joins a double track/old forest road. You descend down the steep gradient through the bottom of the dip and round a right-hand corner. Carry as much speed as possible through this corner into the climb: the climb is not particularly long but the gradient here is pretty steep.

A few metres of flat forest road after the climb gives you a chance to rest the legs and catch your breath. The next section of the trail dips down and climbs up the hillside as you make your way back towards the visitor centre. There are plenty of technical trail features throughout this section to keep you entertained: rock drops, tight corners, blind crests and fast open berms.

The Blue trail will join you from the right and the final kilometre is easier than the previous one. The final section leads you into the open fields by the car park. Continue to follow the waymarkers on the forest road that link back to the visitor centre.

LAGGAN WOLFTRAX

▶**FACILITIES**

Car park and charges: Yes; charges apply

Cafe: Yes

Toilets: Yes

Showers: Yes

Bike wash: Yes

Nearest bike shop: On site

Bike hire: Yes

Accommodation: B&Bs, hotels, self-catering accommodation and camping around the area.

Other trails on site: Green, Black, jump line.

Ordnance Survey map: Explorer 401.

ENJOYMENT FOR SKILL LEVEL

Beginner: 3/10

Intermediate: 7/10

Advanced: 9/10

Getting there: Located just off the A86 that connects the A82 (Fort William) with the A9 (just south of Aviemore), Laggan Wolftrax is just over a kilometre south-east of Newtonmore, past the A889 on the south side of the main road.

Grid ref: NN 59349 92296

Sat nav: PH20 1BU

More info: www.basecampmtb.com

▶TRAIL 1: RED UPPER AND LOWER LOOPS

On-site grade: Red

Clive's grade: Red

Distance: 9km

Technicality: 7/10

Ascent: 382m

ENJOYMENT FOR SKILL LEVEL

Beginner: 3/10

Intermediate: 8/10

Advanced: 7/10

The trail starts on the high side of the car park and climbs up a forest road. At the trailhead you will see some rock slab option lines, these will give you a feeling of the trail ahead. The opening forest road climb continues for approximately 1km before you arrive at the top of the jump line. This line simply shortcuts back down to the car park and can be taken in either now or later in the loop (you will have to climb this forest road from the left-hand switchback one more time).

Near the top of the forest road you will pass a large rock slab to your left. This can be taken in when making your return loop as a Black-option line. At the T-junction continue right and climb up the hillside heading towards the summit at

183

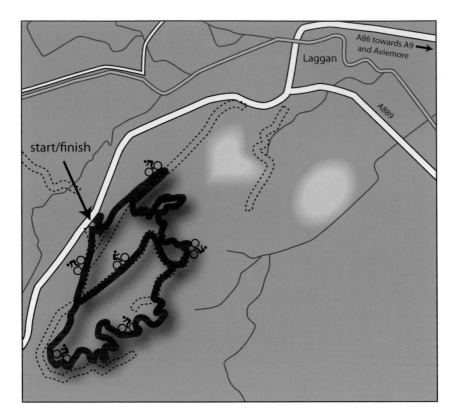

Creag a'Ghrianain (you will turn left at that T-junction on your return loop). Within a short distance, turn left off the forest road and the rest of the climb comprises of a narrow, winding single-track trail.

When you arrive at the top of the climb there is a sizeable outcrop of bedrock to

climb up. On top of this you will see a post and the Black trail straight ahead. The final part of the climb that led you to this point is relatively technical and gives you a good impression of what's down on the Black line, should you wish to ride this.

Turn left into the Red trail and down a swooping single track traversing the hillside. You will come out into open ground and the gradient eases. The trail surface is smooth and it's very easy to maintain a decent pace through the section that flattens out. There are some small drops and jumps with option lines but nothing too major. The single track will sweep back into the treeline rejoining the Black trail.

You will see the Black-option line down this slab on your return leg

This section is a little bit more technical than the previous one and will require some focus and commitment.

You will be on familiar ground now as you climb back up the forest road you started the ride with. After you have made the switch round to the right pass the rock slab once more and turn left at the forest road junction signposted for the return loop. After a few more metres of climbing turn left and start to make your descent. You still have a few kilometres to go and the mellow gradient is made entertaining with rock slabs and drops, there are also some nice turns throughout this section and a few switchbacks complete the line up.

A short forest road link will lead you to a long traverse heading back towards the car park. This final section gives you the option to take on a long boardwalk section. If you do this take care when you leave the boardwalk as you will be joining the jump line trail where riders might be approaching at speed from your left! The

You're rewarded with some stunning scenery at the top of the main hill

final section of trail follows the jump line back to the car park. This final blast has some good sizeable tabletops that will keep you honest.

The final descent is shared with the Funpark line.: take care when joining this trail as riders may be approaching from your left

MABIE FOREST

FACILITIES

Car park and charges: Yes; charges apply

Cafe: Yes

Toilets: Yes

Showers: No

Bike wash: Yes

Nearest bike shop: On site

Bike hire: Yes

Accommodation: Hotel and bunkhouse on site, B&Bs, hotels, self-catering accommodation and camping around the area.

Other trails on site: Green, Blue, Purple, Orange jump park/skills area, Orange northshore trail, permissive paths and forest roads.

Ordnance Survey map: Explorer 313.

ENJOYMENT FOR SKILL LEVEL

Beginner: 7/10

Intermediate: 10/10

Advanced: 7/10

Getting there: From Dumfries take the A710 Solway Coast road. At the end of a long straight section of road you will see signs pointing you up a narrow drive to your right for Mabie House Hotel. Head up the drive over the speed ramps and take the first turning to your right into the car parks.

Grid ref: NX 95011 70739

Sat nav: DG2 8HB

More info: www.bikingheaven.com

TRAIL 1: PHOENIX TRAIL

On-site grade: Red

Clive's grade: Red

Distance: 18km

Technicality: 6/10

Ascent: 483m

ENJOYMENT FOR SKILL LEVEL

Beginner: 4/10

Intermediate: 7/10

Advanced: 6.5/10

From the trailhead sign in the car park, follow the single track joining on to the tarmac road. Take care here as there might be vehicles approaching from either direction. Climb up the tarmac over the speed ramp and you will come to some white buildings to your right, take a right turn here past The Shed cafe. You will ride through the car park above The Shed and onto a forest road. Within a few metres you will see all trails outbound head out to your left up a smooth single-track trail.

The trail switchbacks and climbs up a small hill joining into a double track. You have to take the tight right switchback and continue to follow the double track up to a fork in the trail.

At the fork take a left turn and climb up a short steep bank. The trail then levels out and you need to head straight on at a fork (there is a sign on the blue post showing outbound and return route direction). You will continue to climb on single track and at the end of this section you will pass over two boardwalks and drop onto a forest road.

At the forest road take a left turn. In a few metres you will see a trail to your right. This is the return exit from the loop you are about to ride. Following the forest road you climb up slightly and the forest road turns into single track. Climb up on the single-track trail – you may find the gradient is quite steep at times. At the top of the hill

Keep right and head straight up the trail on your outbound loop

there is a small crag and a bench next to a dry stone wall. This is a great place to stop and catch a breath. On a clear day there are stunning views out across the estuary to the Lake District.

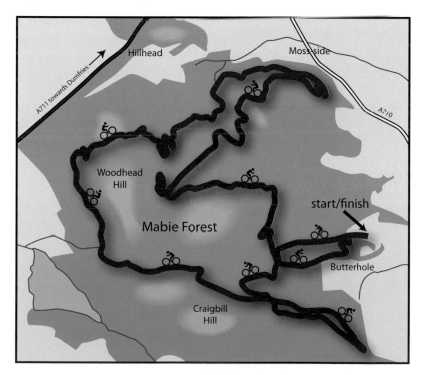

The next section of trail has recently been rebuilt. You will find plenty of interesting features in this trail including small doubles, fast corners, rock drops and various other whoops and jumps. The trail levels out near the lower section and after a short shallow rise you come into a hard right-hand corner. On the exit of the corner, drop down a small crag and into a tight right-hand corner. The trail levels out and one final short drop puts you back on the forest road. Take a left to turn.

Follow the forest road to a T-junction where you take a left turn and climb up the main forest road. You will pass a junction on your right. Continue over the crest of the hill and into a single track to your right. Drop down through a stream splash and the trail climbs up to a pair of switchbacks that lead you into a section known locally as the Handcut. This section has a very natural feeling, there are a few naughty roots and rocky outcrops that you need to negotiate. If you get a chance there are some wonderful views down to your left of Lochaber Loch.

Nearing the end of the section you will cross a small boardwalk beyond which is a rough rocky crag and then a split-line option, to the left the Red trail dips down and takes a right-hand turn around an outcrop of rock, the right option is graded Black and a blind crest leads you into a rocky drop.

The trail then traverses around the hillside and is relatively smooth. This will lead you into a climb through a series of switchbacks. It is worth conserving some energy through the lower parts of this climb as the final section is quite steep and rough.

When you crest the hill the trail dips down and climbs up slightly. In a few metres you have another split-line option. There are no signs here but don't panic as both lines will converge in a few metres' time. The left line merely shortcuts out a

The section of trail that leads to the Contour Climb is known locally as the Handcut. There are some sweet views down to the loch below

The opening section of the Descender Bender has some cool views of the estuary and Solway Coast

corner and rock crag. There is a bench at the top where you have spectacular views back towards Dumfries.

You are now at the top of Descender Bender. This is a fast single-track descent with a good hard-packed surface. The descent is split up into three sections by forest road crossings. Throughout the first section you have a small rock drop before some mellow corners lead you into a large left-hand berm with a hip jump on the exit. This hip takes you into a right-hand berm. A fast section drops you into two right-hand berms with a tabletop nestled in between! If you have never ridden here before it's worth taking a look at these features before you hit them at full speed.

At the bottom of the first section, cross over a forest road and turn left into the next section of descent. This has recently been rebuilt and a series of large berms and fast switchback corners are guaranteed to put a large smile on your face. Partway down there is a small stream crossing. On the

far side a 90° right-hand corner should be approached with caution, the trail surface is loose and it's easy to slide out!

You will cross over another forest road and into the final section of Descender Bender. In this final section there is a small wooden bridge which leads you into a tight right and left hand switchback. After the switchbacks the trail goes back to a more natural feel and a rocky shoot leads you down to the Burn Splash.

After the Burn Splash a narrow single-track trail traverses around the hillside. You will go through a small dip into a short climb, and then another small dip into a short climb. After this the trail goes up a steep bank (this section is known as the Scorpion). At the top of the climb you join a forest road and take a left turn.

With views out to your left towards Dumfries, traverse the hillside for a couple of hundred metres on forest road before taking a right turn and climbing up on a single track. The trail switchbacks up the hill into some large oak trees, this is the start of the Rollercoaster.

The giveaway is in the name: the Rollercoaster dips down and climbs its way around the hillside. On the first section of descent you may want to try and carry some speed into the steep ascent that follows. You will arrive at a forest road crossing (here you have the option to take a shortcut out to your left following the forest road back to the car park should you need to do so). Continue on the other side of the forest road and a short rough traverse links you on to an old forest road.

You get a moment's rest on this old forest road before you enter a single track named Heaven's Gate. A long straight single-track trail drops down between a break in the trees, and a left-hand corner at the bottom leads you into the final traverse around the hill before joining on to another old forest road.

Climbing up on this old forest road you will see the Blue trail pass from left to right. The forest road ends and you need to keep to the right-hand trail, climbing uphill. As you climb up the hillside you will come to a tight left-hand corner. On the exit there is a section of boardwalk that climbs up between two large trees. Beyond the boardwalk the trail traverses around and takes a series of switchbacks climbing up next to a forest road. A very natural steep drop down through some roots gives you a little break from climbing before another section of boardwalk leads you into the final climb.

The Elevator descent (you have just climbed The Elevator climb) is fairly narrow but very fast. There will be a section following a small bomb hole where you come out into the open and a rocky stone-pitched drop leads you into a left hand bermed corner. After this corner an open right-hand corner leads you onto a short section of boardwalk, you then have another series of

The first of two boardwalks in the Elevator climb has a tricky entrance and climbs uphill

fast corners, which take you through some natural bedrock.

There are a few cheeky corners throughout the lower section with a small lip acting as a launch pad into a blind right-hander. Shortly after this you exit a right-hander into a steep climb. This, however, is only short and providing you have selected the right gear and carried some speed you should be able to make light work of it.

After this short climb the trail drops down again and you are now heading to The Bad Step. The Bad Step isn't as bad as the name would have you believe. A good indicator that you are about to arrive at this section is a trail crossing over and the trail you're on levelling out. A stone-pitched drop links you into more single track, just beyond the rock drop there is another set of rocks to drop down. Before these steps you have a short rise, it's the setup here that counts if you want to clear this section with ease.

A series of fast corners drop down to a right-hand switchback where you run parallel to a forest road below you, the trail drops onto the forest road and you follow this for a few metres before dropping left into another section of single track. This section of trail has a very natural feel to it. The surface is heavily eroded, and rocky outcrops and root beds are to be negotiated before you come out of the trees onto another forest road. Take a right turn and immediately turn left onto a double track. Dropping back down to where you started the loop, climb up the steep bank/rocky crag one more time.

Back at the Blue post, where you went straight on earlier on your outbound trail, take a left turn (unless of course you want

The Elevator descent has a few rocky outcrops to contend with

to do another lap) and follow the return trail. The return sections of single track are quite rough and natural feeling, you will cross over a footpath partway along this section and a large root bed precedes the final descent.

Partway down you will cross a small stream. Just after the stream is a cheeky left-hand switchback that can catch a lot of folk out. After the switchback the trail drops down into a series of switchbacks through a pinch fence and onto a double track taking a right turn.

Follow the double track a few metres before switching back to your left and dropping down a rocky and rooty bank. At the bottom of the bank switch round tight to your right and a final few metres of single track link to the quarry drop. If you don't fancy the quarry drop you can always take a left turn and cut around the edge of it.

At this point you should recognise where you are on the forest road as it's where you headed outbound at the start of the ride. Just take a right turn to return to the car park or if you fancy some more fun you can follow the forest road to your left, which will lead you to the skills park/jump area.

▶ SKILLS AREA AND MINI X

The Mini X trail is similar to a 4X racetrack just narrower, you will encounter double jumps, tabletops, rhythm sections, fast bermed corners and a step-up jump. Just below the Mini X trail is a long skinny log ride, if you fancy heading out to The Darkside timber trail then this is a great place to start. In the skills area you will find various features to practise your skills on.

The first tabletop in the Mini X track gives a good kick

Long skinny log rides in the skills area prepare you for Mabie's Darkside

MORAY MONSTER TRAILS

▶**FACILITIES**

Car park and charges: Yes; charges apply

Cafe: No

Toilets: No

Showers: No

Bike wash: No

Nearest bike shop: Gravity Sports Briarbank Westacres, Buckie AB56 5EN Banffshire

Bike hire: No

Accommodation: B&Bs, hotels, camping and self-catering accommodation in area.

Other trails on site: Moray Monster Trails cover a vast area. There are various loops and links. You can park at one of three trailheads to start your ride but unless you want an epic day out you may want to drive to the various trailheads and explore each trail and area individually.

Whiteash car park is located 1km east of Fochabers.

Ordiequish car park is located just over a kilometre south-east of Fochabers.

Ben Aigen car park is located much further south, approximately 4km south-east out of the village of Mulben on the A95. There is a fourth trailhead where you will find a Green taster loop at Quarrelwood.

You will find a variety of Green, Blue, Red and Black-graded trails at the different sites. Each car park has signage advising of the various trails, their grade and distances. Leaflets are available with a well-detailed map of the area showing you the various car parks you can use to ride the trails.

Ordnance Survey map: Explorer 424.

ENJOYMENT FOR SKILL LEVEL

Beginner: 6/10

Intermediate: 9/10

Advanced: 7/10

Getting there: The Whiteash car park is located on the A98 just east of Fochabers. Head north from Keith on the A96 heading to Elgin and take a right turn at a roundabout near Fochabers onto the A96, continue up the main road for 800m and you will see the car park on your right.

Grid ref: NJ 35839 58588

Sat nav: Fochabers

More info: www.moraymountainbikeclub.co.uk

▶ THE FOCHABERS RING TRAIL, STARTING AT WHITEASH CAR PARK

On-site grade: Red

Clive's grade: Red

Distance: 9km

Technicality: 6/10

Ascent: 220m

ENJOYMENT FOR SKILL LEVEL

Beginner: 5/10

Intermediate: 8/10

Advanced: 7/10

From the trailhead signage, head towards the left-hand corner of the car park. The trail opens on a wide double track and runs parallel to the main road for just over 1km. The surface is relatively good, there is just one short section of loose gravel and sand.

You will spend the next few kilometres climbing up towards the monument on the top of the hill. The climb is mainly on double track and there are a few junctions, everything is really well waymarked so you should have no issues in navigating your way up the climb.

The opening sections are relatively uneventful but very pleasant

The gradient is relatively steep in parts and it's advisable to save some energy to enjoy the descent on the return leg. Throughout the upper section you will come across a series of water bars. These are a good indicator your climbing is nearly over.

When you arrive at the monument there is the option of taking a right turn down a more technically challenging downhill trail that shortcuts the far loop of the main Red trail. If you wish to continue outbound on the cross-country loop, simply go straight past the monument and follow the trail ahead.

At the far end of the loop you pass around Gallows Hill and start your return to the car park in a north-easterly direction. You have a few short sections of fast single track with forest-road-link sections to bring you back round to Leitch's Wood and the car park.

This section of trail runs parallel to the A96. It is very natural and can become quite wet and slippery throughout the winter months. You will also have to negotiate root-beds and rough surfaces as you traverse the hillside. Elevation loss is minimal and the trail requires a fair bit

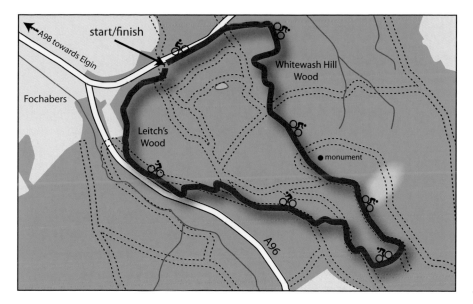

of effort if you wish to maintain a decent speed. It's only when ridden at speed that it becomes technically challenging.

Unfortunately, while on my road trip investigating the trails in this area the weather turned and we had to leave and head south to sit out the passing snow storms. We would love to have had the time to ride the other trails in the area as the Fochabers Ring Trail was only a small sample of what's on offer here. If you visit this part of the UK allow plenty of time to savour the other Monster Trails.

The water bars made from logs are a good indicator that you are nearing the top of the first climb

The trails are narrow and very natural feeling

NEWCASTLETON

▶ FACILITIES

Car park and charges: Yes; charges apply

Cafe: No

Toilets: Yes

Showers: No (but there is a changing room)

Bike wash: Yes

Nearest bike shop: BikeSeven, Unit 2, Sandilands, Longtown, Cumbria, CA6 5LY (01228 792497)

Bike hire: None on site

Accommodation: B&Bs, hotels, self-catering accommodation and camping around the area of Newcastleton village.

Other trails on site: Blue, Purple, skills area/taster loop, permissive paths and forest roads.

Ordnance Survey map: Explorer 324.

ENJOYMENT FOR SKILL LEVEL

Beginner: 6/10

Intermediate: 8/10

Advanced: 4/10

Getting there: From the A7 at Longtown head north towards Langholm. At the village of Canonbie, take the second right turn and drop into the village centre. Turn left and head north-east on the B6357 to the village of Newcastleton. Just as you enter the 30mph limit you will see brown signs pointing you right up a lane over the river. Head straight on up the lane and follow the narrow lane through a series of tight corners up the hill to the car park on the right.

Grid ref: NY 50170 87397

Sat nav: Newcastleton

More info: www.7stanesmountainbiking.com

▶ TRAIL 1

On-site grade: Red

Clive's grade: Blue with Red sections

Distance: 15.5km

Technicality: 4/10

Ascent: 275m

ENJOYMENT FOR SKILL LEVEL

Beginner: 4/10

Intermediate: 8/10

Advanced: 4/10

At the far end of the car park pass through the gate in the dry stone wall and take the right turn, climbing up the forest road. At the top of the forest road you will pass a junction to your left – this is your return route. For the outbound trail continue straight ahead until you see signs directing you to take a single track on your right-

Choose your trail

Chainsaw art

hand side. This is where you will find the skills area/taster loop. The Red trail takes in a few jumps before levelling out and climbing up slightly, a series of switchbacks drop you into the first part of the descent.

The trail has been cut into a terraced hillside. The majority of the opening 2km is descending, however there are a few uphill sections and steep ramps to break up the fun. Partway through the section you will cross a forest road. The lower section opens with a natural trail and runs down by some large oak trees, there are a few bridges to pass over throughout the section and care should be taken on wet days. At the bottom of the descent you will switch left on a forest road and traverse along next to Tweeden Burn.

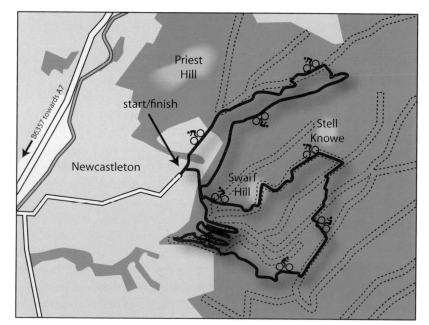

Gullies are traversed with boardwalks as you near the bottom of the first descent

The border stone

A long forest road section steadily climbs upwards with the river down to your left. You will arrive at a T-junction with the Borderstone to your left. This section forms part of the link with the trail over at Kielder Forest and makes for quite a long epic ride. Take a left turn and run along a long straight section of forest road before a section of single track on your left cuts through the trees, crossing over Tweeden Burn once more. The bridge over the burn is quite narrow so riders with wide handlebars will have to take care. Beyond the bridge the trail climbs up the hill through a series of steep switchbacks.

The climb joins a forest road. Turn right and. within a few metres, take a left turn into another section of single track. Once again you climb up the hillside. The gradient here isn't as steep as the previous section. You join a forest road at the top of

Dead Man's Quarry climb and a short flat section links you to a T-junction where you take a left turn and climb up. The forest road levels out and you will get a short section of single track on your left-hand side. There are some fast corners in this section so take care as the surface is quite loose.

A short forest road links to the next single track on your right. Switchback up the hill in the trees, passing the quarry viewpoint and into the descent. The gradient through the downhill isn't particularly steep but the smooth trail surface makes it easy for you to carry a decent speed. There are a few rough sections that only last for a couple of metres at a time. There are also plenty of fast corners throughout this section and you will drop back down, linking to the forest road you headed outbound on earlier.

Taking a right turn onto the forest road and then another right turn along a forest road link, the next sections are shared with the Blue trail. You will cut across the top of the Dun Knowe to a turning circle where you enter a single-track descent. There are some tight corners in this section and the surface is loose. At the bottom of a short descent, join a forest road link. A fork left puts you into a short single-track climb.

Traversing the hillside you will come to a series of tight switchbacks and onto a wooden boardwalk. After the boardwalk some more fast corners link you to a wooden bridge as you cut across the hillside. At the end of the section you drop down through a series of switchbacks and onto the forest road. Follow the forest road which joins into a tarmac road and within a kilometre you're back at the car park.

A smooth trail traverses open ground

The return traverse is shard with the Blue trail

IRELAND

BALLYHOURA

► FACILITIES

Car park and charges: Yes; charges apply

Cafe: No

Toilets: Yes

Showers: Yes

Bike wash: Yes

Nearest bike shop: On site

Bike hire: Yes

Accommodation: B&Bs, hotels, self-catering accommodation and camping in the surrounding area.

Other trails on site: Five loops of various lengths. Each loop is an extension of the one before it.

ENJOYMENT FOR SKILL LEVEL

Beginner: 4/10

Intermediate: 6/10

Advanced: 6/10

Getting there: From Dublin take the N7 onto the M7, heading south towards Limerick, then pick up the M8 towards Cork. Come off at junction 12 and take the second exit to the N73, heading towards Kildorrery. Take a right turn in the middle of town onto the R512. After 12km you will see a sign pointing you up a narrow lane to the left to Ballyhoura Forest.

Grid ref: R 652 191

Sat nav: Kildorrery

More info: www.trailbadger.com

► TRAIL 1

On-site grade: None given

Clive's grade: Red

Distance: 35.5km

Technicality: 5/10

Ascent: 740m

ENJOYMENT FOR SKILL LEVEL

Beginner: 2/10

Intermediate: 5/10

Advanced: 6/10

There are no grades applied to the coloured arrows

Unlike elsewhere in the British Isles, the trails in the Republic of Ireland have not been given a grade. Here at Ballyhoura there is a series of trails made up from purpose-built single-track sections linked by forest roads.

At the far end of the first loop you have the option to extend your ride and take in the second loop. Halfway round the second loop you again have the option of extending your ride and taking on a third loop. You can do this for five consecutive loops, making for a grand day out, and adding up to more than 50km of riding.

The trials are colour-coded but the colour does not reflect any particular grade: you'll find a green, brown, white, blue and red trail. Each trail is made up from single-track sections, double tracks and forest roads. You will encounter technical trail features, tight corners, tough climbs and spectacular views.

We rode a combination of the green,

There are great views on all the loops

brown, white and blue trail. This made for a good solid ride. There was nothing too intimidating out there, but a novice rider might find some sections hard work. If you're unsure, ride the initial loop and see how you get on. When you get to the first split you can cross-reference the trail signage and see if you want to take on the next loop.

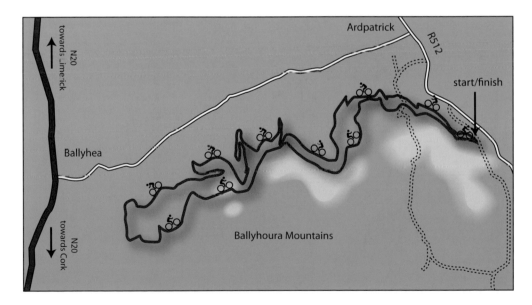

Spectacular views over Limerick

Boardwalks and narrow trails twist around the forest and hillside

You will find where each loop links into the next as there is a trailhead sign giving you a good indicator of what lies ahead. The information given includes distance and elevation as well as a rough description of what to expect under wheel.

It seems that mountain biking on the Emerald Isle has finally been accepted and embraced by private landowners and local authorities. The mountain biking scene is booming on the island and this can only be a good thing. By the time you read this there will probably be more purpose-built trail centres across Ireland for you to discover.

BLESSINGBOURNE

▶FACILITIES

Car park and charges: Yes; charges apply

Cafe: No

Toilets: Yes

Showers: No

Bike wash: Yes

Nearest bike shop: Real Cycles, information available on site

Bike hire: Yes

Accommodation: On site self-catering cottages. B&B, hotels and camping around the area.

Other trails on site: Pump track, estate roads.

Getting there: From the A4 heading west into Fivemiletown, you will see a large sign saying 'Bike at Blessingborne'. Turn right at the small roundabout, take a tight left-hand corner then right again.

After a few hundred metres you will see a small entrance on your right signposted for the trails.

Grid ref: NV 55327 11872

Sat nav: Fivemiletown

More info: www.blessingbourne.com

▶TRAIL 1

On-site grade: Blue

Clive's grade: Blue

Distance: 5–6km

Technicality: 3/10

Ascent: 72m

ENJOYMENT FOR SKILL LEVEL

Beginner: 10/10

Intermediate: 7/10

Advanced: 4/10

Blessingbourne Manor

The main trail starts next to the pump track

From the car park the trail heads out through a young plantation of pine trees. Here the surface is smooth and the going easy. You will run parallel to the public road climbing uphill and twisting around trees towards the church. The trail levels out and

you start to descend. Some of the corners tighten up and the surface is loose if you go off the ride line.

You come out into open ground and have stunning views of the lake and the manor house over to your left. The trail then joins a double track where you climb up slightly before taking a right turn into a section of single track. You twist your way around and will see the Red return trail to your left. Continue straight on where you enter a Red-graded section. You will find a skinny log ride and option lines that take in rolling rock drops. The trail joins a double track before another section of single track turns off to the left.

After a few metres you will come to a split in the trail. The left line drops back down towards the Blue trail and you can repeat the last section again, or to follow the main loop take a right turn. You will

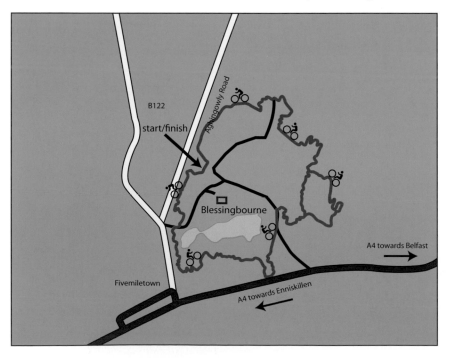

Tranquil trails in stunning scenery

descend down through a series of corners and tabletops. Crossing over one of the estate roads at the bottom a Red-graded single track twists its way through the trees.

A short link on double track put you into the final Red section of trail. There is minimal elevation loss and gain here and the trail surface means it's very easy to carry speed. At the end of this section you will join a Blue-graded trail which links back to the car park.

There is a network of estate roads and it is very easy to make up a much longer route by taking some of the fun single tracks more than one time.

You'll also find next to the car park a pump track. Riding the pump track is a fantastic way to improve your technique and provides a good warm-up before heading out for a blast.

Rock drop-option lines for those of you who need that extra challenge

ROSSCAHILL

▶FACILITIES

Car park and charges: Yes; free

Cafe: No

Toilets: No

Showers: No

Bike wash: No

Nearest bike shop: MBW, Unit 5, Moycullen Business Park, Moycullen, Co Galway (353-91 556525)

Bike hire: No

Accommodation: B&Bs, hotels, camping and self-catering accommodation in and around the area.

Other trails on site: Natural trails and forest roads.

ENJOYMENT FOR SKILL LEVEL

Beginner: 3/10

Intermediate: 7/10

Advanced: 8/10

Getting there: From Galway head west to Clifden on the N59. Take a right turn just as you enter Rosscahill signposted for Brigit's Garden. The car park for the trails is on your right in just under 1km.

Grid ref: M 178 380

Sat nav: Rosscahill

More info: www.trailbadger.com

▶TRAIL 1

On-site grade: None given

Clive's grade: Red with Black sections

Distance: Various., our loop was 6km

Technicality: 8/10

Ascent: 80m

ENJOYMENT FOR SKILL LEVEL

Beginner: 3/10

Intermediate: 7/10

Advanced: 8/10

There is a large network of natural single-track trails here that can be connected by forest roads. The sections of single track and forest road can be ridden in any direction and order. You're likely to encounter other trail users so take care when descending and joining on to trails and forest tracks.

Although there is minimal elevation to this area, the trails themselves will make you work hard. There are smooth chunks of rock and large boulders strewn all over the trail. The soil can become quite soft and sticky and lots of sections will be tough work on a wet day.

You will find the occasional arrow and sign but there is no obvious loop. It is worth taking either a paper map or GPS units and spending a few hours getting your bearings to find out what's where and how to link up all the available trails.

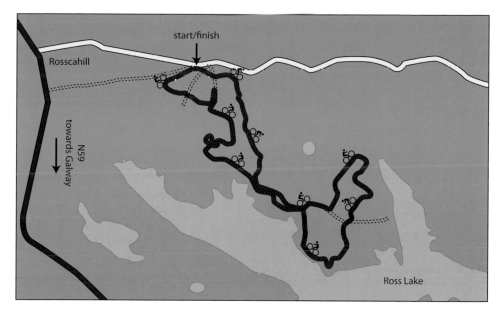

To get to the first section of single track from the car park, head round the gate and down the forest road until you see a climb to your left. This links you into a ridge line in the trees. Here there are multiple options and trails running off in all directions. If you follow your nose in this general direction you can't go wrong.

You will find our short 6km route available on the Garmin connect website.

Technical climbs may be short but there are plenty of them

Testing natural trails are all over the forest

ACKNOWLEDGEMENTS

To my dearest Daria, you have been an inspiration beyond words and I'm so proud to be your husband, here's to many more adventures in the years to come.

To my brother Kevin and his family.

Thank you to Piera, Maurizio, Giorgia and Valerio, my new found family.

A BIG thank you to all my sponsors, Kevin, Kyle, Sam, Lars and the folks at Transition Bikes US. Graeme, Sean and the staff at SurfSales. Jimmy at MuleBar, Dominik at Osprey, Simon from Garmin UK, Ian at CTC, Stephanie at Stena Line, Neil from Surface Clothing, all the guys and girls at Exposure Lights, Blacks Outdoor, John at G&G/The Shed, Mark at Next Level, Matt at Chaineys Cycles and Steve at iCycles for the coffee.

Special thanks to Danny, Ric and the guys at Mountain Biking UK magazine.

Becky and all the folk in Future towers. Mark Huskisson and family, Ad. Jane and the Bates family and the kind folk at Blessingbourne manor for the hospitality.

Once again to all my friends for there continued support, Gav, Pip, Beeg, Caz, Jockey, Fev, Seddon, Rob, Robbie, Skinner, Tally, Wendy, Jemma, Rachel, Potsy, Big Mark, Ian and Andy 'its a Wednesday' Marshall, Lyle, Williams, Youth, Aston, James McKnight, Dave & Ginger Marshall, Big Dave at MyOsteo and family. Far too many of you to list, thanks for the friendship and support.

Huge thanks must go to Frazer, my comrade-photographer on the rides, without whom there would be no book.

A final thank you to Charlotte, Nick and all the folks at Bloomsbury Publishing, thank you once again for the opportunity.

INDEX

Note

Whilst every effort has been made to ensure that the content of this book is as technically accurate and as sound as possible, neither the author nor the publishers can accept responsibility for any injury or loss sustained as a result of the use of this material.

Published by Bloomsbury Publishing Plc
50 Bedford Square
London WC1B 3DP
www.bloomsbury.com

First edition 2013

ISBN (print): 978-1-4081-7944-4

A CIP catalogue record for this book is available from the British Library.

Acknowledgements

Cover photographs © Frazer Waller and Shutterstock
Inside photographs © Frazer Waller
Maps by Tom Croft
Commissioned by Charlotte Croft

This book is produced using paper that is made from wood grown in managed, sustainable forests. It is natural, renewable and recyclable. The logging and manufacturing processes conform to the environmental regulations of the country of origin.

Typeset in 9.5pt on 13pt Myriad Pro by Margaret Brain, Wisbech, Cambs

Printed and bound in China by C&C Offset Printing Co

10 9 8 7 6 5 4 3 2 1